LA Scavenger

I0806430

Danny Jensen

REEDY PRESS

Reedy Press
PO Box 5131
St. Louis, MO 63139, USA
www.reedypress.com

Library of Congress Control Number: 2022949034

ISBN: 9781681064314

Cover and interior design by Claire Ford

Cover and interior photos by Danny Jensen; interior clip art courtesy of Pixabay and Wikimedia Commons.

Printed in the United States of America
23 24 25 26 27 5 4 3 2 1

Dedication

To my incredible wife, Adrienne.
Thank you for all your love and support.

Contents

Acknowledgments vii
Introduction viii
Olvera Street 2
Chinatown 14
Downtown 22
Little Tokyo 36
Boyle Heights 44
Highland Park 50
Pasadena 56
Echo Park 64
Silver Lake 70
Los Feliz 76
Hollywood 86
North Hollywood 96
Koreatown 102
Leimert Park 110
Miracle Mile 116
Fairfax District 124
West Hollywood 130
Beverly Hills 142
Westwood Village 150
Culver City 156
Santa Monica 166
Venice 174

Acknowledgments

Thank you to the people of Los Angeles—past, present, and future—whose stories and dreams enrich this beautiful landscape. Thanks to the entire Reedy Press team for helping to bring this book to life. Much thanks to my family and friends for their support and encouragement, including Kris Miller, who joined for some of my research excursions. I'd like to thank and acknowledge the Indigenous peoples that have long inhabited and continue to inhabit this land, including the Tongva, Kizh, Chumash, Serrano, and Tataviam (Fernandeño). I'd also like to thank the Los Angeles City Historical Society, the Los Angeles Public Library, the Los Angeles Conservancy, the California Historical Society, the Chinese Historical Society of Southern California, the Little Tokyo Historical Society, the Boyle Heights Historical Society, the Highland Park Heritage Trust, the Pasadena Museum of History, the Echo Park Historical Society, the Silver Lake Heritage Trust, the Los Feliz Improvement Association, the Hollywood Heritage Museum, the West Hollywood History Center, the San Fernando Valley Historical Society, the Museum of the San Fernando Valley, the Valley Relics Museum, We Love Leimert Park, Save Beverly Fairfax, Miracle Mile Residential Association, the Beverly Hills Historical Society, the Beverly Hills Conference and Visitors Bureau, the Culver City Historical Society, the Santa Monica History Museum, the Santa Monica Conservancy, the Venice Historical Society, and many other museums and cultural institutions which provided a wealth of information and support to me while I researched this book.

Introduction

They say that nobody walks in LA, but with this book in hand, you'll ditch the car and discover Los Angeles' hidden treasures that you'd otherwise zip past. The sprawl of LA may seem daunting, but it's that expansiveness that makes it such an exciting place to live and visit. As someone who has explored and written about LA for over a decade, including for my first two books, *100 Things to Do in Los Angeles Before You Die* and *Secret Los Angeles*, I've certainly found that to be true. The sheer size of the city and county allows so many amazing, eclectic neighborhoods to develop their own distinctive personalities. Meanwhile, the vast landscape offers everything from sandy beaches to rolling hills to beautiful mountain trails. The challenge, however, is knowing how to navigate that huge, diverse landscape. And that's where this book comes in.

Los Angeles Scavenger invites visitors, recent arrivals, and longtime Angelenos alike to explore Los Angeles neighborhood by neighborhood to find famous local landmarks. Rhyming clues and photos will serve as your guides to help you identify notable locations that help tell the story of the neighborhoods and Los Angeles at large. The clues will offer visual hints to help you in your quest, along with a bit of history or fun facts about the place. The landmarks include historic buildings, public art, and museums, as well as iconic restaurants and businesses.

While LA has a reputation as a car-centric city, for these scavenger hunts you're encouraged to ditch the car and walk or roll to find these locations. You'll find most of the clues centered around the core of each neighborhood on one or two main streets, except for a few landmarks that might be a little farther off the beaten path. Once you find one clue, the next won't be too far away. All the neighborhoods are accessible by public transit and have parking options available.

While some of the neighborhoods could be explored in an afternoon and others in a full day, I encourage you to take your time in tracking down the clues over multiple days, if possible. Not only will you get to savor your victories as you locate each landmark, but you'll also have the chance to find other fascinating places and really get to know the neighborhood. It's easy to get caught up in our daily routines, rushing from one location to the next. This book gives you the excuse to wander leisurely, open to uncovering new places and hidden gems or to gaining a deeper appreciation for familiar spots. Don't forget to look up, down, and all around in your search to find details you might otherwise miss.

One of the biggest challenges of writing this book was narrowing down which neighborhoods and landmarks to feature and which to leave out. With all those amazing, eclectic neighborhoods across LA, and the rich history and culture found within each one, the decisions were difficult—but I couldn't include every neighborhood and every landmark. My hope is that you use this book as a springboard to explore more of LA and to always be on the hunt for the hidden places that make a place special, wherever you travel.

Good luck, and enjoy the adventure!

Legend

1 Olvera Street
2 Chinatown
3 Downtown
4 Little Tokyo
5 Boyle Heights
6 Highland Park
7 Pasadena
8 Echo Park
9 Silver Lake
10 Los Feliz
11 Hollywood
12 North Hollywood
13 Koreatown
14 Leimert Park
15 Miracle Mile
16 Fairfax District
17 West Hollywood
18 Beverly Hills
19 Westwood Village
20 Culver City
21 Santa Monica
22 Venice

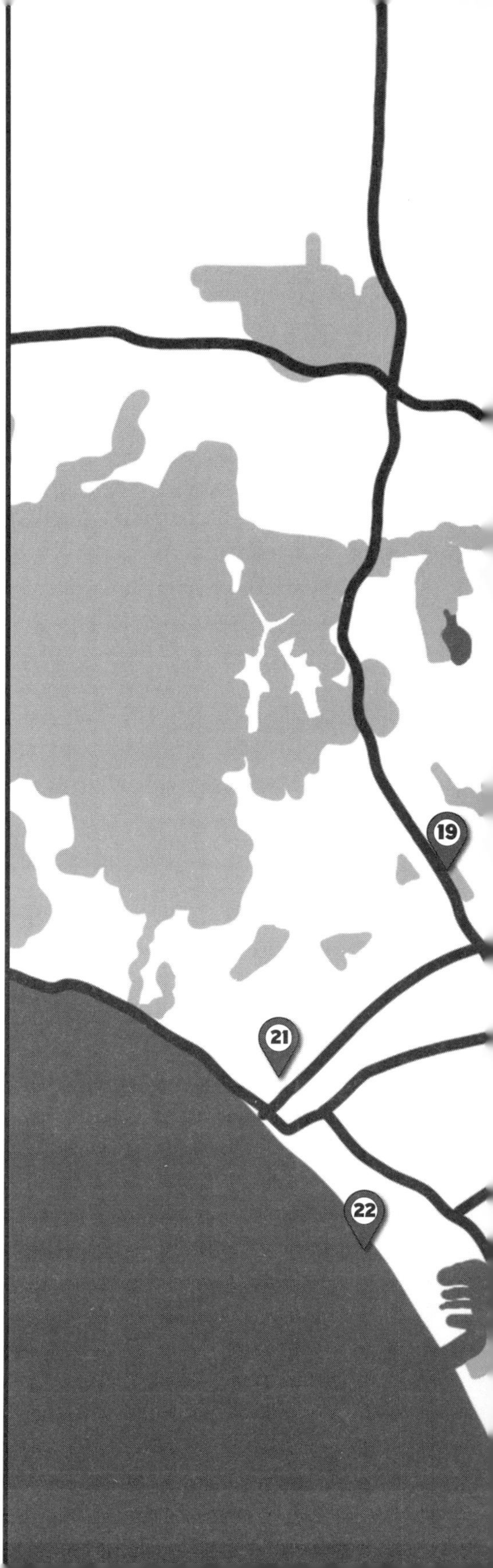

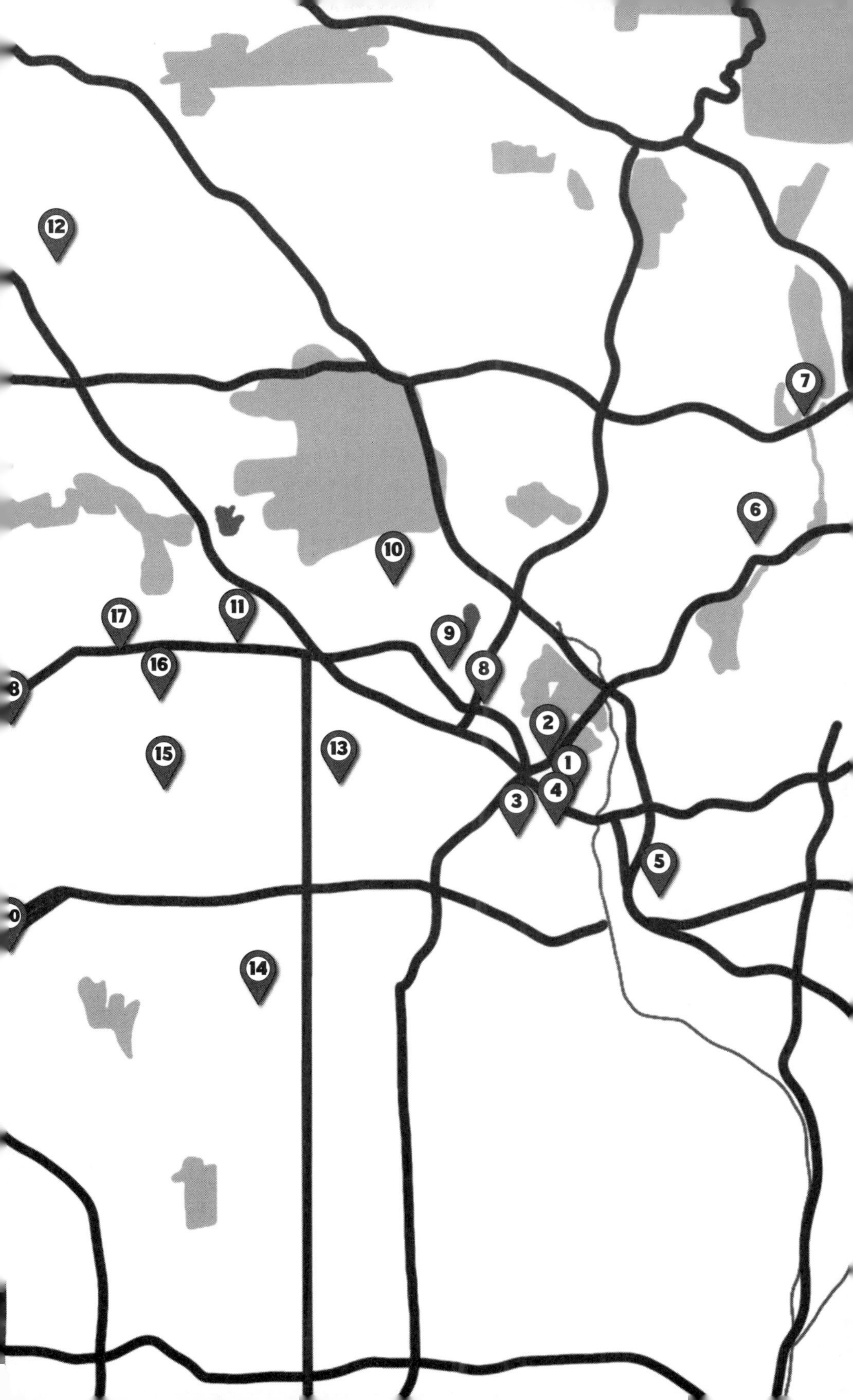
12
7
6
10
11
17
9
16
8
2
13
1
15
4
3
5
14

Olvera Street

Considered the birthplace of Los Angeles, El Pueblo de Los Ángeles Historical Monument is a vibrant, living museum. Here, you'll find some of the oldest surviving buildings in LA, a variety of fascinating museums, and plenty of places to eat and shop. Los Angeles was founded here in 1781 as El Pueblo de Nuestra Señora la Reina de Los Ángeles de Porciúncula, one variation of LA's early names. But for thousands of years prior, the area was part of one of the largest villages of the Tongva people (also known as Gabrieleño, Gabrielino, and Kizh) who still live in the region. While Olvera Street was developed in the 1930s by Christine Sterling as a romanticized version of the Spanish colonial era, the effort did help preserve the area, and it has since evolved into a popular destination for locals and visitors. Take Metro B Line (Red) or D Line (Purple) to Union Station. Metered parking and lots are available.

1

LA's oldest theater that stands today,
Italianate in style with green and gray
Once held masked balls for LGBTQ:
It now stands vacant with grand plans in view.

2

A lengthy mural painted green and blue
Of early LA gives a sweeping view,
An ancient tree stands above the pueblo,
First known as Yaangna where river did flow.

3

LA's first "skyscraper," five stories high,
Built 1888, bricks toward the sky.
Named for a drug company, looks quite smart,
And now it's a home for culture and art.

4

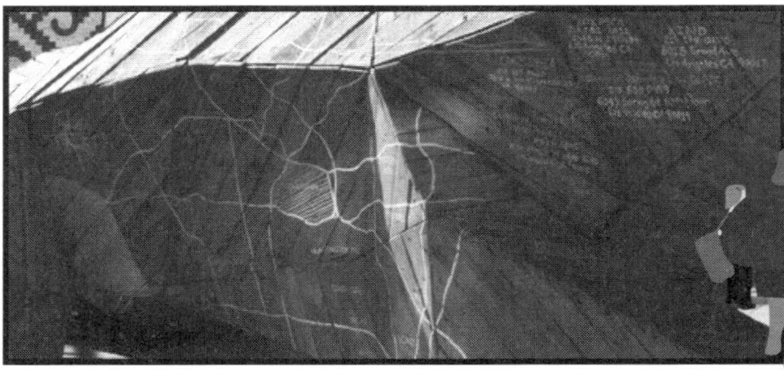

While this wood coyote won't give a yelp,
Its map and numbers offer migrants help,
New homes on its back for those who arrive,
Donations by its tail to help them thrive.

5

Built on the site of a mission from Spain
1814, LA's first to ordain
The Queen in mosaic, the angels hail,
Nearby, the bell from a historic trail.

6

LA's first three-story building's not slim,
A former luxe hotel now with blue trim.
The last governor of Mexican rule
Built this grand house, an Italianate jewel.

7

Round the bend or an alley, you'll go down
The last survivor of Old Chinatown,
The two-story brick, oldest of that time,
Learning the history won't cost a dime.

8

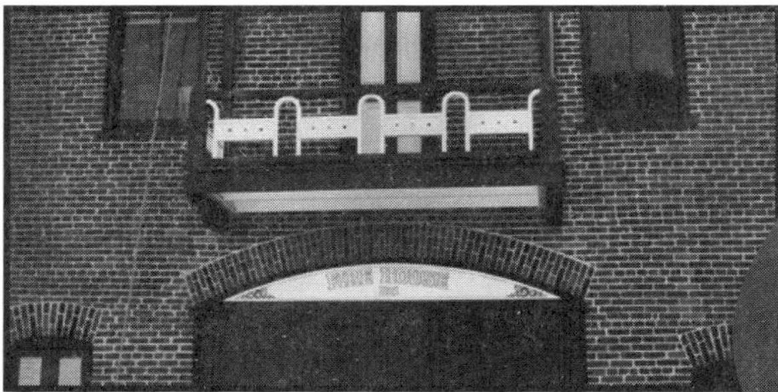

LA's first building for fighting the flame,
Restored in the '60s, it looks much the same:
A belfry up top and a porch in green,
Inside barn doors, vintage wagons are seen.

____

____

9

A tradition as old as the city,
To miss this mural would be a pity.
For a blessing, the livestock they would bring,
Now with pets, tradition lives on each spring.

____

____

10

Before fame, he slept on benches nearby,
Now in bronze, the immigrant's head held high,
El Charro de Mexico rides his steed,
An icon of music and film, indeed.

11

Circles in bronze, 11 names in all,
Of those families, 44 made the haul.
Close to the spot where the river did flow
"Queen of Angels," they founded the pueblo.

12

It stands on circles of flowers and stone,
Tribute to when the pueblo was first known.
Though the first wore out from weather and rot,
A new one was carved by artist Hadnot.

13

The oldest home that still stands in LA,
Its thick white walls are made of sunbaked clay.
A mayor once stood on its porch of wood,
Inside, history will be understood.

14

White brick, green trim, a balcony above,
The boarding house kitchen, history buffs love.
See the front on Main, in the Eastlake style,
Enter on Olvera: the tour's worthwhile.

15

LA's oldest house of fired brick stands here,
The cellar was used for wine and not beer.
Painted in white with red porch down below,
A sign tells of sherry, not of Bordeaux.

16

Food and a workshop through this brick archway
Where Italians made wine back in the day.
There's an ancient grapevine just overhead,
From when Olvera was Vignes instead.

17

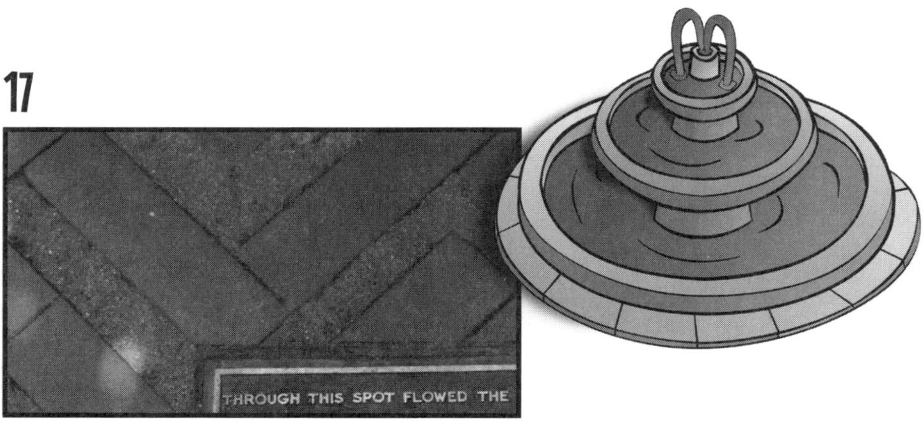

There's a blue fountain surrounded in stone,
Where brick zigzags, the "Mother Ditch" is shown,
Water from the river to the pueblo
Flowed through this channel and helped it to grow.

18

A home to athletes back in '32,
Yellow clapboard with red trim is your clue.
The first Olympic village: Baldwin Hills
Moved one here, sells ponchos with frills.

19

Where now there are stairs, just above stained glass,
Find the sign and faded stills that most pass.
This famous film was shot in black and white;
Here, the orphan and the Tramp reunite.

20

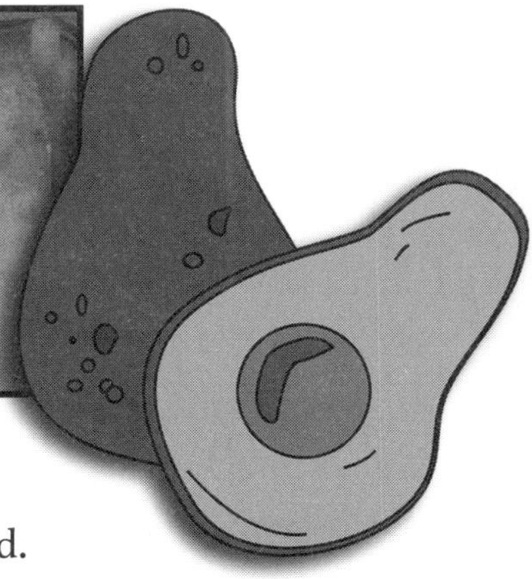

Always a line, this red and orange stand
Sells taquitos, famous throughout the land.
One of the oldest restaurants in LA,
Avocado salsa will make your day.

____

____

21

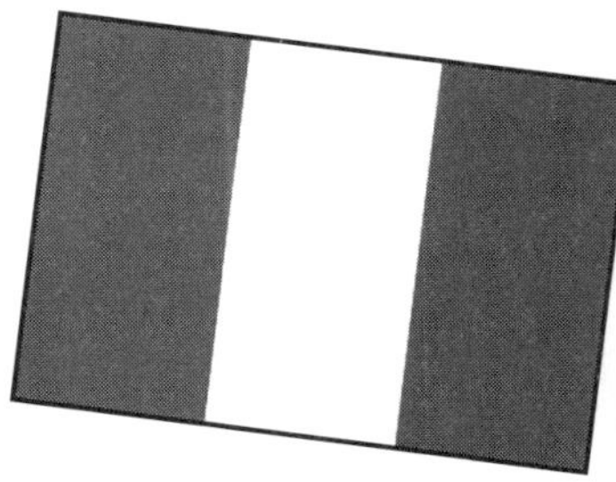

Head around to Main Street and you shall see
Part of LA's own Little Italy,
A historic hall with mosaic tile,
The museum inside is worth your while.

____

____

22

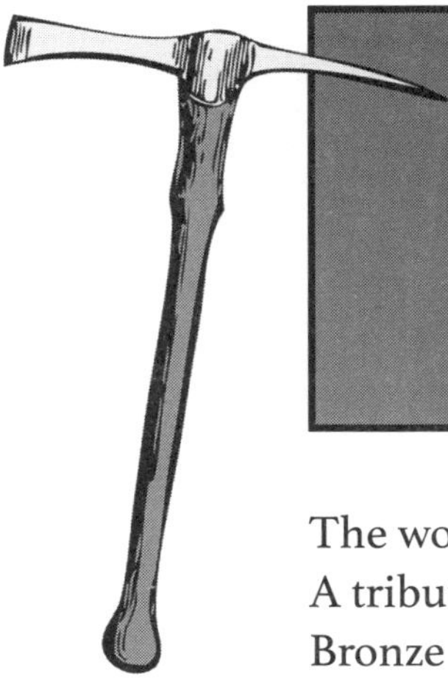

The worker stands tall, family left behind,
A tribute to migrants who farmed and mined.
Bronze tools and barbed wire, cross for those lost,
Mexican laborers paid a great cost.

23

The last great terminal of world renown
Once was the site of old Chinatown,
Mission moderne with arches and tower,
To find public art, be sure to scour.

Chinatown

Located north of Olvera Street and south of Dodger Stadium, Chinatown is one of LA's smaller neighborhoods, but there's still plenty to explore. While LA's first Chinatown was razed to make way for Union Station, the "New Chinatown" that you see today opened in 1938 and still features its now-iconic design elements: colorful pagoda-style roofs, red lanterns, and pedestrian plazas. You'll find plenty of delicious spots to eat, both new and old, as well as art galleries, charming shops, and frequent street festivals. Take the L Line (Gold) to the Chinatown Station. Street parking and lots are available.

1

Two golden dragons soar high overhead,
They bring good luck and harmony, not dread:
Red flames at the elbows, pearl in between,
In the clouds below, a mist can be seen.

2

Two floors with a green-tiled roof and red trim,
With amazing food, it's filled to the brim.
Rising-star chefs and classic spots abound;
Down the hall, culinary gems are found.

3

The blue sign with neon is your first tip
To find the origins of the French dip.
It was first opened in long-lost Frenchtown;
The hot mustard is the best, hands down.

4

Dragons on the roof, and by the front door
An incense altar with ornate decor,
A tribute to the goddess of the sea,
On Lunar New Year, it's the place to be.

5

Just down the stairs from the Gold Line station,
A replica from another nation.
Two thousand years ago, the first one rang;
A symbol of peace, you can see it hang.

6

Curved concrete, orange and yellow both sides,
World's largest gang rehab, turning the tides,
Jobs, training, tattoo removal, and more,
A fantastic café at the front door.

7

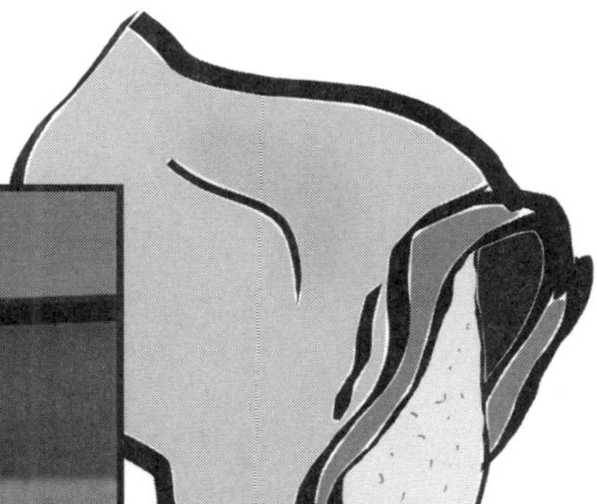

A bald eagle where they once milled flour,
Zanja Madre's water supplied power,
Grinding since before 1883,
Now restaurants, shops, and offices you'll see.

8

With so much greenery, it might be hard
To picture this as a former train yard,
Now art, an orchard, and paths can be found,
See Zanja Madre's bricks, just above ground.

9

Though there's no longer water for the fish,
If you've got spare change, here's where to wish.
The Seven Star Caverns inspired its look:
You'll find Buddha and others in each nook.

10

Yellow and black, a balcony above,
Once a music venue rock fans loved.
The "Godmother of Punk" was Madame Wong;
Here's where now-famous bands played their song.

11

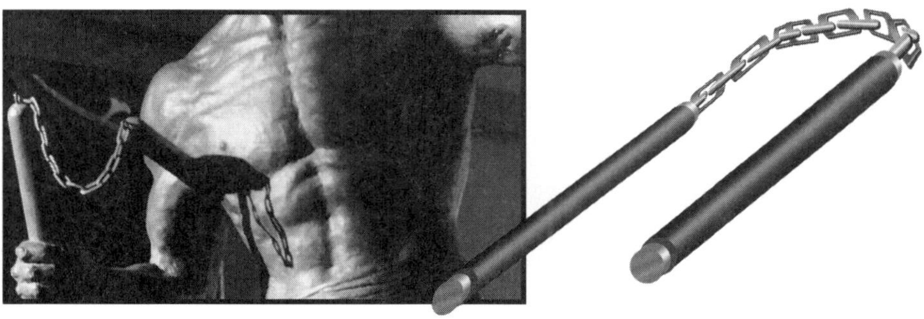

Seven feet of bronze poised, ready to fight,
A martial arts legend stands day and night.
His Jeet Kune Do studio once nearby,
Pose with this film star before you pass by.

12

Balcony red, yellow, and blue, with green tiles,
Wood shelves lined with words in a range of styles,
Volumes new and old, music, art, and more,
For activists, a printing press in store.

13

Since '38 it's been baking up treats,
Loved for strawberry cakes and Chinese sweets.
The artist who inspired *Bambi* designed
The shy mascot with a package behind.

14

Two single-story Queen Annes, side by side
Painted purple with porches, hard to hide,
What's inside now won't be a mystery:
It's Chinese American history.

15

The huddled masses in concrete and steel,
Behind the abstract figures, a train wheel,
Allegory for triumph and struggle,
Which newly arrived immigrants juggle.

Downtown

While Downtown LA was sadly neglected for decades, the area has undergone an incredible transformation and is once again a thriving place to explore. Whether you're looking for innovative restaurants, swanky hotels, historic architecture, prominent museums, or live music and sports, Downtown has you covered. Much of your scavenger hunt centers around the Historic Core, as well as Bunker Hill and the Civic Center. Take Metro's B (Red), A (Blue), D (Purple), or E (Expo) Line to 7th Street/Metro Center or the B or D Line to Pershing Square or Civic Center/Grand Park Station. Metered parking and lots are also available.

1

Blue-yellow-tiled domes, balconies you'll find
Cali's first female architect designed,
Mission revival for Hearst's newspaper,
Now restored, not torn for a skyscraper.

2

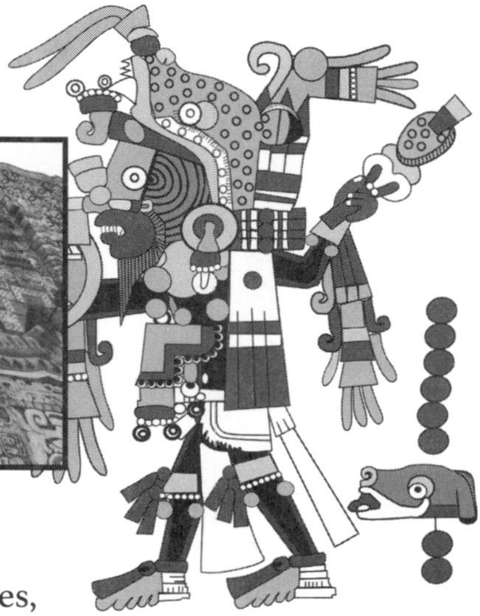

Mesoamerican-inspired designs
Beneath the marquee are often long lines,
Lavish carvings in blue, green, red, and gold,
Seven ancient figures, sight to behold.

____

____

3

Gothic gem by legends of Hollywood,
Since '27, this building has stood,
Terra-cotta figures above the door,
Now a hotel, restaurant, theater, and more.

____

____

4

Turquoise terra-cotta, trimmed blue and gold,
Clock tower and name in neon, quite bold,
Clothing was once sold, now lofts on each floor,
Look for the sunburst above the front door.

5

LA's first "talkie" film was shown here,
Now it's where the latest tech will premiere,
Renaissance details, a prominent clock,
Portraits by locals run along the block.

6

Marquee says "diamonds," but there's more in store:
A Warner Brothers theater made crowds roar.
Where once the old logo, now there's a jewel;
The beaux arts design makes architects drool.

7

Vintage wood paneling and bright neon sign,
Since 1932, LA's come to dine,
Bars and cafeteria, newly restored,
Where history lives and you're never bored.

8

An alleyway runs between jewelry and clothes,
Small, hidden restaurants: follow your nose!
European façades, colors so bright,
A college and Bullock's once stood on this site.

9

Baroque Spanish arches soar up above,
For great food options, a tunnel of love.
A vaulted skylight connects the two sides,
Let the griffins above serve as your guides.

10

Floral flourishes above the front door,
A former bank with surprises in store.
Literary labyrinth, tomes old and new,
Last of its kind, there's music and art, too.

11

Through a black fence, see walls covered with art,
Here, a dark history has a fresh start,
Native Americans found support here,
Now murals by native artists appear.

12

Five-acre plaza, once called Central Park,
Redesigned many times, it's still a landmark,
Named for a commander in the Great War,
Find a bronze doughboy who fought in the corps.

13

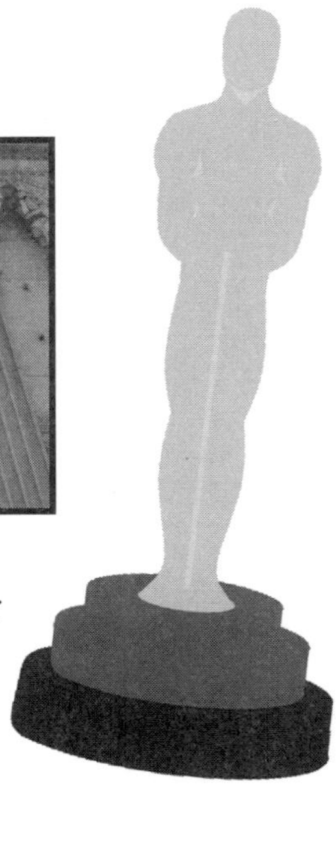

Three Beaux Arts towers with Renaissance flair
Hosted the Oscars, and Beatles stayed there.
Ceres and Neptune perch above the door,
The seal of LA is part of the decor.

14

On its pyramid, the sun always shines,
Just be sure to avoid overdue fines.
Literary figures carved in limestone,
Torch on top symbolizes all that's known.

15

A sculpture of orange stairs: your first clue,
Behind the plaza, two doors are askew,
Tall, black, and bronze with art deco design,
Saved from a tower gone from the skyline.

16

Perched on the corner, stands out from the rest,
First electric heat and cooling out West.
Front rotunda crowns the deco motif,
Find symbols of power in bas-relief.

17

Its white honeycomb shell, known as the "veil,"
Filters natural light on a huge scale.
A cyclops' eye reveals a "vault" of art,
Century-old olive trees look quite smart.

18

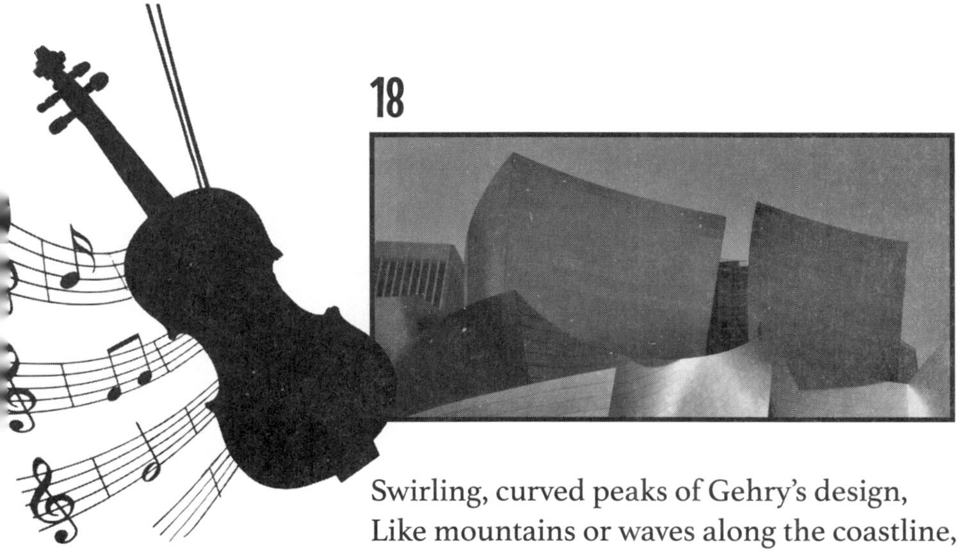

Swirling, curved peaks of Gehry's design,
Like mountains or waves along the coastline,
Shimmering steel swoops the audience in,
Look around for the Blue Ribbon Garden.

19

Step through the archway, you're on the right track:
A funicular in orange and black.
Sinai and Olivet are quite a pair;
They'll spread their wings to fly you way up there.

20

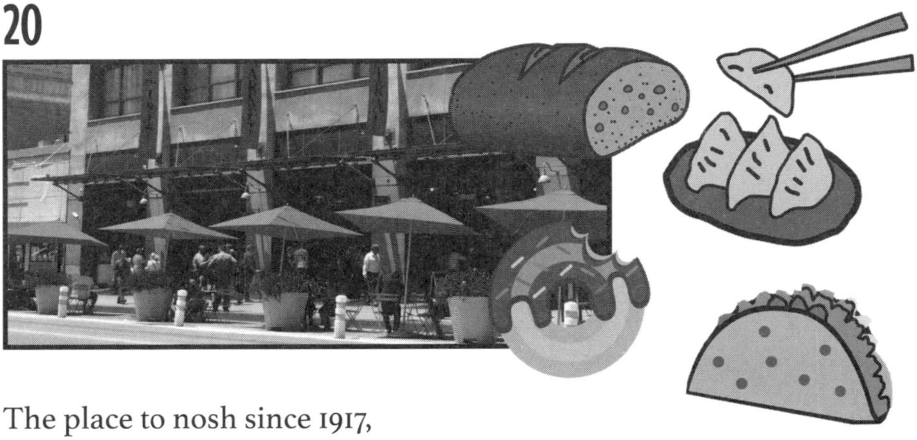

The place to nosh since 1917,
Its rows of food vendors are labyrinthine.
Enter on Broadway or stroll in on Hill,
At this grand old food hall, you'll get your fill.

21

Grauman's palace named for its rumored cost,
LA's first grand theater has not been lost.
Elaborate archway above the marquee,
Above Muses of Arts, bison you'll see.

22

Oldest commercial building in LA,
Its name on the terra-cotta archway.
While the five-story brick building's subdued,
By the atrium inside, you'll be wooed.

23

Between Broadway and Spring hides a small park
Named for an influential matriarch.
The wall tells of her remarkable life,
Pioneering Black woman and midwife.

24

Although the presses all stopped years ago,
This deco fortress is still one to know.
Two limestone eagles perched up by the clock,
The name carved on the side, seen down the block.

25

With a mausoleum-inspired rooftop,
When illuminated, the colors pop.
For decades, the tallest building for miles,
Observation deck will surely bring smiles.

26

Close to where the trees of City Hall sway,
A tall post with blue signs that point the way.
Though the mileage may suggest a long trip,
With each place, LA shares a close kinship.

27

Its three wishbones inspired by a church nave,
Stained glass prisms create a rainbow wave.
Its spaceship-like form once synced sound and light:
With support, it could once again shine bright.

Little Tokyo

Located between Downtown's Historic Core and the Arts District, Little Tokyo is a charming neighborhood that's rich with Japanese American culture and history. You'll find a wide array of restaurants and shops, historic temples, public art, and several museums. Be sure to spend time wandering around Japanese Village Plaza, the pedestrian mall that makes you feel like you're exploring the streets of Japan. Take Metro's L Line (Gold) to Little Tokyo. Metered parking and lots are available.

1

Look up for a sign where jazz greats once played,
For "Bird" and Miles into wee hours, they stayed,
Once one of Bronzeville's breakfast clubs that swung,
They closed postwar, so they're often unsung.

2

Tall columns flank this former house of prayer,
A united place for worship and care.
While war took the congregation away,
Now artists have found a place they can play.

3

The shop to go for DIY repair,
Plus, chefs and gardeners will find treasures here.
The wooden doors might be easy to miss,
But carved stone up top is just the chef's kiss.

4

Inside this sweet and quaint, historic shop,
There's colorful mochi that's worth a stop.
Run by the family since 1903,
A line of fans is the first thing you'll see.

5

Once known for stir-fry that couldn't be topped
And neon that thankfully wasn't chopped,
Now it's the place for small bites and craft beer:
The bar may seem far, but in fact, it's quite near.

6

Above the crowds soars this tower,
Painted boldly the color of power,
Known as yagura in rural Japan,
If fire was spotted, here they would plan.

7

Giant Rubik's Cube that you can rotate,
Designed to combat prejudice and hate.
Thirty diverse faces here become one;
You'll even see your own when it is spun.

8

A pillar of stone, engraved, marks the way
Down a narrow alley, a place to pray,
Bonsai, stone, and bronze welcome the devout,
Over a century Buddhists sought out.

9

On three tall legs stands a large, wood-like box,
This device captured stories behind locks,
Handmade with a lens that was snuck within,
Photos showed what shouldn't happen again.

10

A stone doorway stands opposite one of glass:
This is where Buddhists once gathered en masse.
It's now a museum where we can see
Japanese American history.

____

____

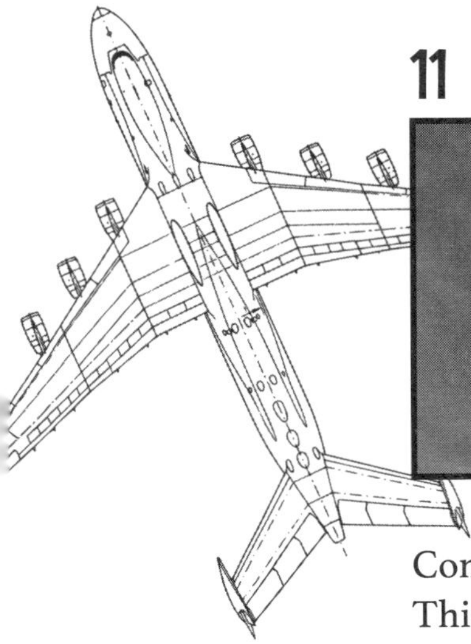

11

Composed of steel wire and salvaged parts,
This hulking sculpture is among the arts.
Is it a bird? Or maybe it's just planes?
Balancing junk must have taken great pains.

____

____

12

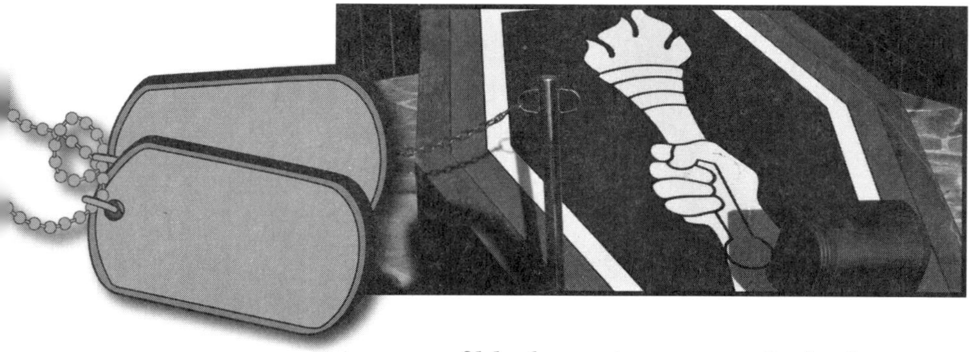

A curve of black granite surrounds the flag,
The names of heroes, each wore a dog tag,
They fought for the country, did so with pride,
Even though their own rights were still denied.

13

It might be a challenge to find this space,
A shuttle placed over a smiling face,
A model tribute to heroes we lost,
Seven names that paid the ultimate cost.

14

Two fiberglass tubes, they twist and they turn,
Unity between cultures, you'll discern,
A symbol of friendship twisted in knots,
The artist leaves us to connect the dots.

15

This secret garden is tucked down below,
A peaceful escape for those in the know,
A babbling stream and wandering walk,
Maybe a wedding or a place to talk.

Boyle Heights

Just east of Little Tokyo and across the LA River, Boyle Heights was once known as the "Ellis Island of the West," thanks to the successive waves of first-generation Angelenos. You'll find excellent food, street art, and cultural landmarks that reflect the Latino, Jewish, Japanese, African American, and other communities that have lived in the area over the years. Catch the L Line (Gold) to Pico/Aliso or Mariachi Plaza Station. Metered parking and lots are available.

1

Connecting the neighborhood to Downtown,
You can see the river if you look down.
Five pairs of Roman-style arches, each side,
A bronze plaque honors an engineer who died.

2

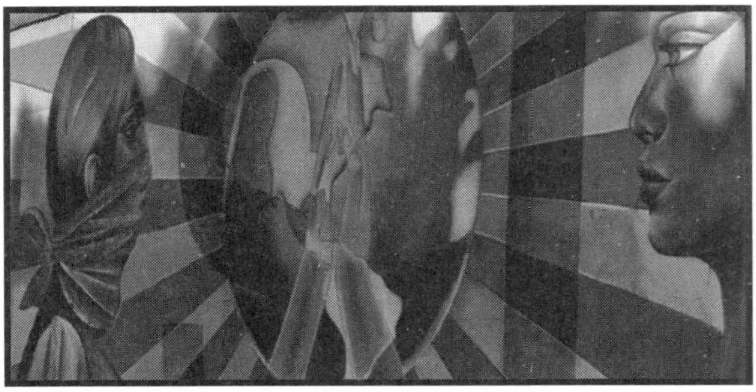

Two palms unite, best seen from a distance,
Tribute to an Indigenous resistance.
Inside, Chicano and Latinx art,
A gallery and classes where you can take part.

3

At a train station where tracks have been laid,
Beneath three canopies that offer shade,
Twenty-seven faces in iron are cast,
Members of the community amassed.

4

Brick building and turret with bell-shaped top,
First floor, a lending library bookshop,
A hotel built in 1889,
Now affordable housing, restored shine.

5

A gift from Jalisco, hand-carved in stone,
Blue-tiled dome, St. Cecilia stands alone.
Tuscan-style columns, a stage for the band,
To hear mariachi, here's where to stand.

6

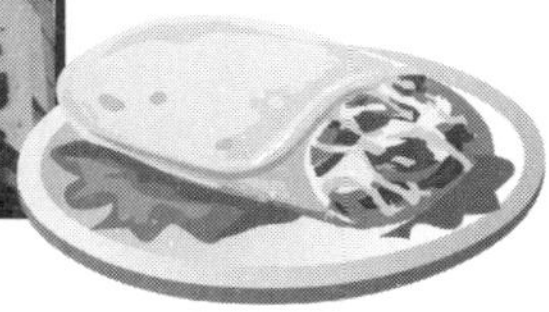

A simple brown awning, a couple's name,
Tiny burrito stand with big acclaim.
A neighborhood icon since '66,
It's the place to get your bean and cheese fix.

____

____

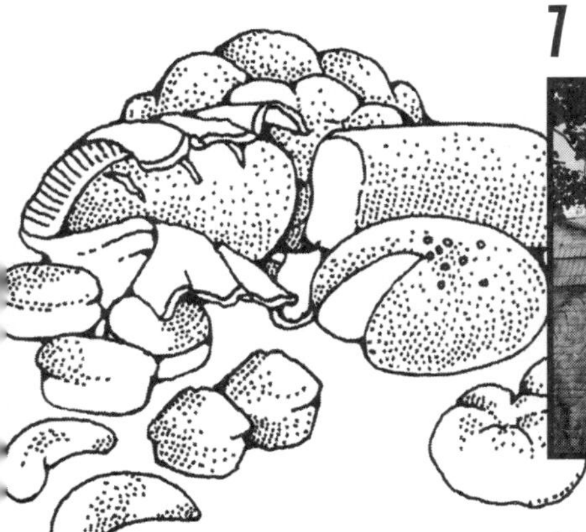

7

Century-old pharmacy with acclaim,
With the Gateway City, it shares a name.
Famous murals on the side and in back,
Inside, vegan baked goods for a snack.

____

____

8

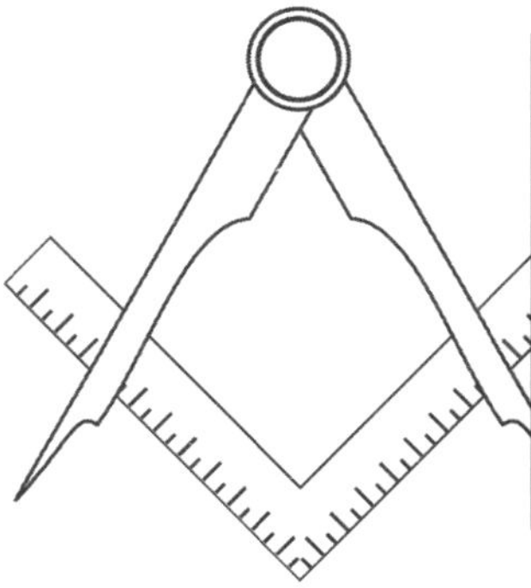

Masonic symbols above ornate door
Show what this civic building was built for.
Was once used by Chavez and Huerta, too,
The red-tiled roof also serves as a clue.

9

Up Breed Street stands a historic landmark,
Stained glass 'neath the arch, bricks light and dark,
A centerpiece of Boyle Heights' Jewish past,
Now a community hub that will last.

10

Here lies LA's oldest burial ground,
Where famous and diverse names can be found.
Stone Gothic chapel built 1903,
Around the grounds, a jogging path you'll see.

____

____

11

Look for large characters in a red font,
LA's oldest Japanese restaurant,
Green slats on the windows, yellow façade
For its homestyle cooking, many applaud.

____

____

Highland Park

Northeast of Downtown LA and southwest of Pasadena, Highland Park is a historic neighborhood and one of LA's earliest suburbs. You'll be searching for landmarks around York Boulevard and Figueroa Street, which feature great architecture, trendy and long-standing restaurants and bars, and eclectic shops. Be sure to also check out the Southwest Museum, the Lummis Home, and the Heritage Square Museum. Take the L Line (Gold) to the Highland Park Station. Metered parking and lots are available.

1

The strings are always attached in this place,
And it's sure to leave a smile on your face.
Catch a performance beneath the marquee:
These puppets aren't just for kids, you shall see.

2

The Cape Cod shingles and ceramic tile
Give this venue a most peculiar style.
Transformed from the seedy club that was here,
It's now the place for locally brewed beer.

3

For fans of old-school and hard-to-find pop,
This old-world grocery store is where to stop.
Vintage candy and beer also line shelves;
At the fountain in back, folks help themselves.

4

This Renaissance Revival is the place
To learn about the cops and robbers chase.
Vintage squad cars and uniforms abound;
The city's oldest station you have found.

5

Near a library with a stone tower
Stands the pole that first delivered power
Throughout the city in 1916.
On the ground, a historic plaque is seen.

6

Mythic feathered serpent across the wall,
The work of 10 artists, sure to enthrall,
Indigenous cultural scenes portrayed,
Vivid message of unity conveyed.

____

____

7

Above where you'd make a deposit, look:
Colorful scenes out of a storybook.
A Millard Sheets-designed mosaic frieze,
See children riding horses through the trees.

____

____

8

Its green and white bulbs light up in the night;
Since '24, this venue has shone bright.
Spanish-style, a balcony on the side,
Lewis A. Smith designed: there's local pride.

____

____

9

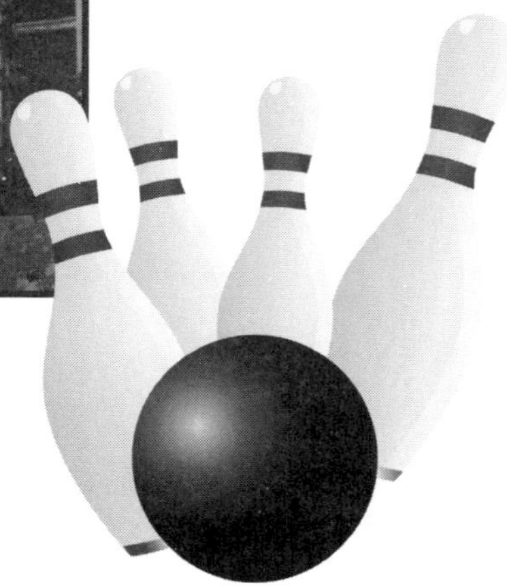

Beneath the neon of a pin and ball,
You will find the oldest lanes of them all.
The historic façade remains the same,
But restored inside for a vintage game.

____

____

10

A colonnade balcony providing shade,
While the frieze above shows tools of the trade.
Italian Renaissance designs in brick,
Once a temple, now a lodge to frolic.

11

This fine feathered friend stands proud on the roof,
Bucket in hand, blue-jeaned boy is no goof,
He's LA's own Statue of Liberty,
This fowl proves we can be fun and free.

Pasadena

Northeast of Downtown LA and part of the San Gabriel Valley, Pasadena is the second-oldest city in the Los Angeles area. This scavenger hunt will take you through some of the spectacular mansions of Millionaire's Row, the art and architecture of Old Pasadena, and the many great shops and restaurants centered around Colorado Boulevard, which was once part of the historic Route 66. Take the L Line (Gold) to Memorial Park. Metered parking and lots are available.

1

Iconic Craftsman home perched on a knoll,
The house you can tour, the grounds you can stroll.
Brown shingles, beams above porches for sleep,
Behind Doc Brown's garage, gardens to peep.

2

White, sphere-topped posts with a green, metal gate
Where history and a mansion await.
Pasadena's stories are on display,
Folk art and a grand home down the pathway.

3

This seated bronze sculpture is deep in thought,
By a famous French artist it was wrought.
Near the museum door, more of his art,
Compared to this one, perhaps none as smart.

4

Whether fans of chewing gum or baseball,
This millionaire's home has something for all.
Known also as Tournament House, you'll see,
Tour acres of roses and house for free.

____

____

5

More than metaphor, where two roads diverge,
You'll see a utensil start to emerge,
At 18 feet, a larger-than-life pun,
Once guerrilla art, now official fun.

____

____

6

To have a proper cuppa and a snack,
Find a horseless carriage and Union Jack
With tea, scones, and all things British in store:
Even royalty has passed through the front door.

7

Moorish domes and Spanish tiles on the roof,
The first built in the city that was fireproof.
Once the annex of a sprawling hotel,
Find the enclosed bridge of this citadel.

8

Yellow stucco walls and a roof red-tiled,
Now you'll find pizza where baggage once piled.
Once the historic train station, Del Mar,
Now it's a bustling restaurant and bar.

9

The heads of two local heroes in bronze
Broke racial barriers as sports icons.
The accomplishments of these two brothers,
Etched in their hair to inspire others.

10

Beaux Arts style with a cupola-topped dome,
Grand arches like what you might see in Rome.
Baroque fountain in the garden courtyard,
On the west side, see fierce lions stand guard.

11

An ornate frieze above windows rounded,
Lending before the city was founded,
There were two other versions built before,
Plenty to "check out" inside to learn more.

12

This plaza offers a quiet retreat
Where water channels zigzag at your feet.
Find the rose on the mosaic tile walls,
Nearby, Batchelder tiles where water falls.

13

Beijing palace designs with a courtyard,
On the green-tiled roof, antique dogs guard
A home with galleries behind arched door,
Now a museum with artwork and more.

14

It's the official theater of the state,
Since '17, crowds it will captivate
Spanish colonial with a courtyard,
First to produce all the works of the Bard.

15

Red awnings and a newsstand in the front,
For favorite authors, you won't have to hunt,
SoCal's oldest independent seller,
For bookworms, the selection is stellar.

Echo Park

Southeast of Silver Lake and west of Elysian Park (home to Dodger Stadium), Echo Park is a dense neighborhood full of history and hidden gems. You'll be exploring locations around Echo Park Lake (where echoes were heard during its construction, allegedly giving the area its name) and along Sunset Boulevard. Along the way, you'll encounter cool shops, great restaurants and food trucks, music venues, and more. Be sure to check out the beautifully preserved Victorian homes along Carroll Avenue in nearby Angelino Heights, one of LA's oldest neighborhoods. Take Metro Bus 2 or 603 to Sunset/Alvarado, 4 to Sunset/Park, or 92 to Glendale/Reservoir. Free and metered street parking and lots are available.

1

She welcomes you to the lake, palms face out,
Icons at her feet, behind her a spout,
By Ada May Sharpless, deco concrete,
The Queen of the Angels stands 14 feet.

2

A copper-trimmed lighthouse and Spanish tiles,
Giant swans to paddle, but no crocodiles.
Built in '32 to replace the first,
Grab a quick bite or quench your thirst.

3

An Olympic mural from '84,
Restored by the artist who's painted more,
Two staircases meet with multiple flights,
Enjoy a view of the lake and more sights.

4

Floating on water, pink, yellow, and white,
When they blossom in summer, quite a sight,
A yearly festival, everyone goes,
Who planted these sacred blooms? No one knows.

5

A bronze bust on top of a concrete block
Faces away from the path that most walk.
Cuban revolutionary and poet,
Placed in '76, most don't know it.

6

Massive dome covered in abalone shell,
Curved façade, imposing columns as well.
Sister Aimee opened in '23,
The first megachurch still draws crowds, you'll see.

7

Gray and black fins on the deco marquee,
Here, vaudeville and silent films you could see,
Now named for a curve and a nearby street,
With local craft beers and plenty to eat.

8

Up-and-coming bands play this dual venue,
But the space was once known for its menu.
Old sign remains from the immigrant hub,
Went from Mexican restaurant to nightclub.

9

"Whenever you are, we're already then,"
In this time-defying shop, grab a pen.
Robots meet cavemen at this charming store,
The writing workshops are never a bore.

10

No relation to me, but shares a name,
Once the place for bowling or a pool game.
Red brick, terra-cotta tiles white and blue,
Now the guy bowling a strike glows anew.

11

Thirty-two bronze plaques within the concrete,
The names of sports stars who couldn't be beat,
Local legends, Olympians, and more,
By a Dodgers photog who knew the score.

Silver Lake

Wedged between Los Feliz and Echo Park, the neighborhood of Silver Lake is centered around its namesake pedestrian-friendly lake (in fact, an artificial reservoir). This scavenger hunt is focused primarily along Sunset Boulevard with its boutique stores, chic restaurants and coffee shops, and hidden painted staircases. While the hilly neighborhood has become known as a trendy destination, it also has a deep history as a Latino, Asian, and LGBTQ enclave, as well as a home for musicians and artists. Take Metro Bus 2 or 4 to Sunset/Silver Lake or the B Line (Red) to Vermont/Santa Monica. Metered and free street parking is available.

1

Two roof peaks topped with rows of window frames,
For indie rock, one of the biggest names,
Once home to taxidermy and trolleys,
Now a courtyard with jacaranda trees.

2

Pastel purple and peach you can't miss,
This slice of Cuba feels sun-kissed,
Strong coffee, fresh pastries, and Cubanos,
Trip to Havana, just follow your nose.

3

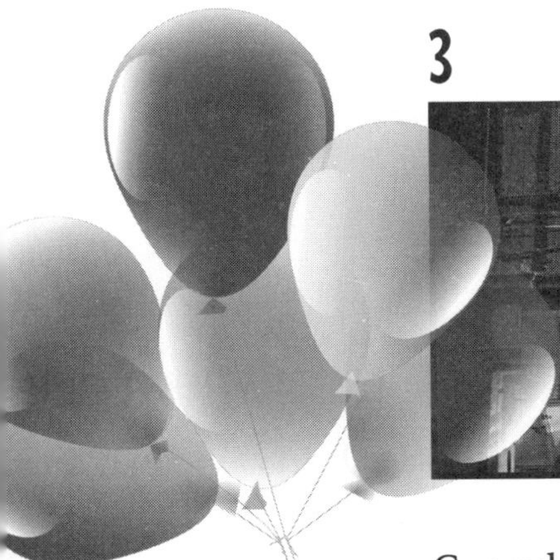

Curved building and arches with neon proves
Disco to cumbia, it's got the moves.
Translated from Spanish, it means balloons,
Dance until dawn and hear all kinds of tunes.

4

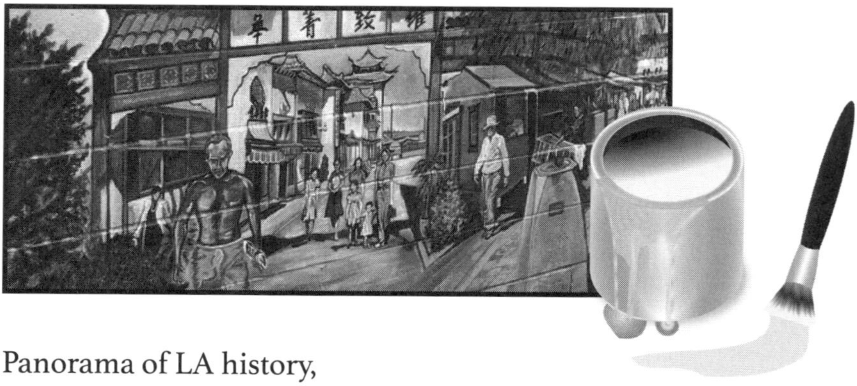

Panorama of LA history,
To some, the walker is a mystery,
But those who knew his green shorts and long route
See this mural as a fitting tribute.

5

Just down Vendome, find these musical stairs
Used by one of film's best comedic pairs.
Laurel and Hardy, though try as they might,
Struggled with a piano on each flight.

6

Just across from a school with the same name,
Vibrant colors and hearts give these stairs fame.
To get to streetcars the steps were handy,
Now a great workout, and dubbed "Stair Candy."

7

The spot for hearty fare since '26,
Sidewalk seats or spinning stools, get your fix,
Put a song on the jukebox while you wait,
They serve breakfast all day: you'll clean your plate!

8

This art deco building painted in white
Is named for a feline that's dark as night,
After a midnight raid, violent arrests,
Historic LGBTQ protests.

9

Here's where two crosstown streetcars would meet,
This iconic sign is still there to greet.
Though Silver Lake is two words and not one,
This star-studded sign is still pretty fun.

10

Thirteen verdant plots zigzag down the hill,
Since '04, growing veggies and goodwill,
The smallest community in LA,
Once you smell the flowers, you'll want to stay.

11

Yellow stucco and shields are entrancing,
A Spanish theme with flamenco dancing,
Sip sangria and, for the dancers, cheer,
The prison-themed Jail Café once stood here.

Los Feliz

The laid-back, strollable neighborhood of Los Feliz is just east of Hollywood, northwest of Silver Lake, and south of sprawling Griffith Park. You'll explore tree-lined streets featuring eclectic restaurants and unique bars, funky independent shops, and historic homes. The hunt will take you along Sunset and Hollywood boulevards and up Vermont and Hillhurst avenues, but you'll also explore Barnsdall Art Park and neighboring Little Armenia and Thai Town. Catch the B Line (Red) to Vermont/Sunset. Free and metered street parking is available, along with a few lots.

1

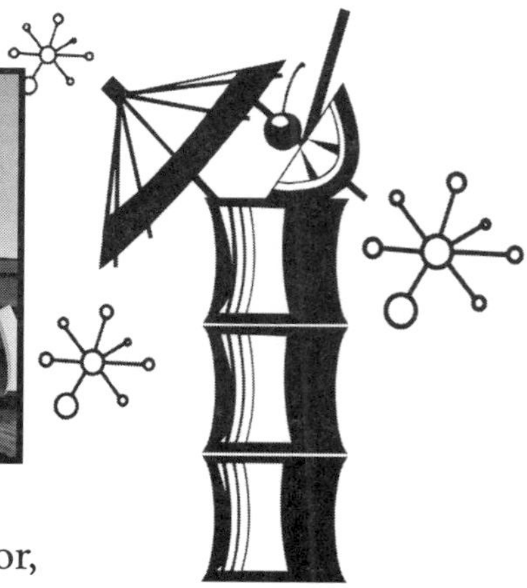

A glass buoy hangs above the front door,
A beacon for the thirsty washed ashore,
Potent drinks and tropical kitsch await,
Since '61, the place to celebrate.

2

Spanish Revival designs worn with pride,
The marquee displays what's playing inside.
The prints of the stars are found at your feet,
Grab some popcorn before you take your seat.

____

____

3

Wacky neon and wild murals stand out,
Curved windows with a border leave no doubt,
Not just soap, but gifts, toys, and books sold here:
In the gallery, new artists appear.

____

____

4

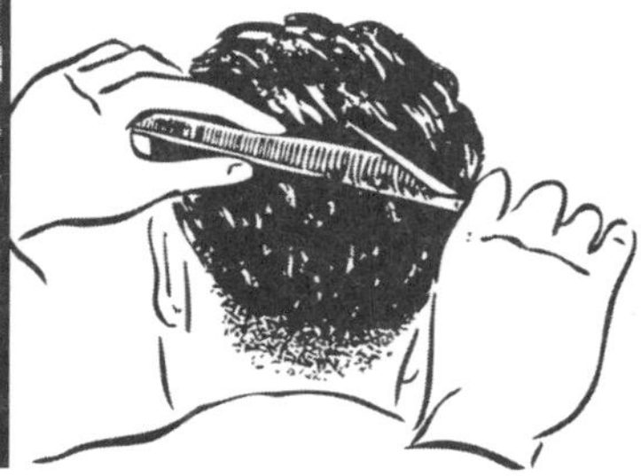

For a shave and a cut, you've found the place,
This old-school spot will frame your face.
The spinning pole will catch your eye;
Just be glad they don't serve meat pie.

5

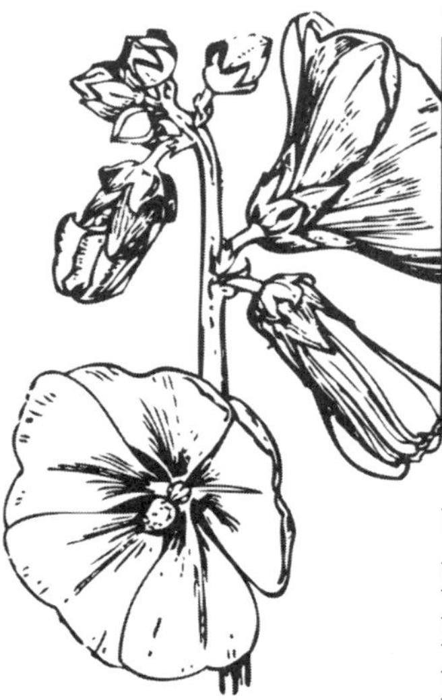

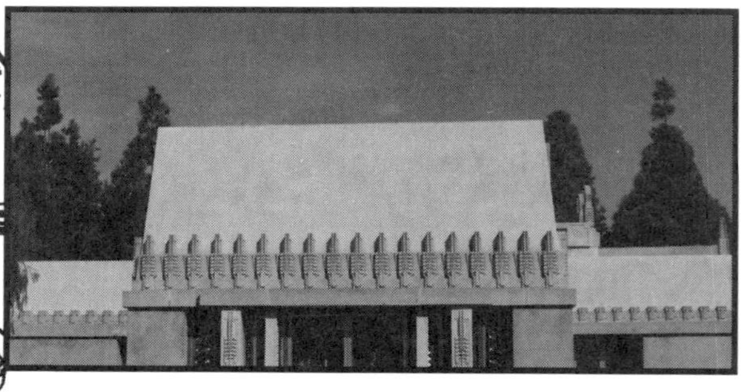

Up the hill is a house that's quite a sight,
Named for a flower and designed by Wright,
Restored to its glory, it's worth a tour,
Its park has a view, theater, art, and more.

6

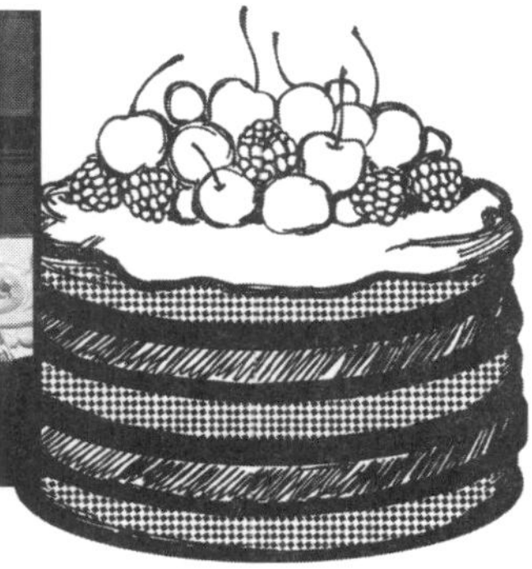

The white, ornate molding looks just like cake,
Much like the Italian pastries they'd make.
Neon tells of a family business gone,
The venue has changed but music lives on.

7

Vanity lights frame the Germanic name,
This iconic bar and restaurant of fame,
Mustachioed man and stained-glass windows,
Live music inside, you'll stay until close.

8

More gifting than trading at the small store,
Custom T-shirts, fun mugs, tchotchkes galore,
Peer inside to see a famous street sign,
Two feet: one sad and one doing just fine.

9

From great staff picks to your favorite 'zine,
Lit from above, a Ficus in between,
Theater next door and annex down the block,
You might just hear a beloved author talk.

10

The bright neon glows in purple and green,
Three panels announce what plays on each screen.
Since '34, its tower has stood tall,
It's a silver-screen gem, welcoming all.

11

Fresh fruit or cream, all with a flaky crust,
A shingled home where dessert is a must,
Sole survivor of a regional chain,
Key lime to pecan, may it always reign.

12

Its ribbed golden domes soar up in the air:
Since ’69, its group’s gathered for prayer.
The windows echo the domes, if you look,
Regardless of faith, a free meal they’ll cook.

13

Red and white awnings shade patio seats,
This celeb favorite serves Italian eats.
Brick and tile façade gives a timeless look,
When they learn it’s not that old, most are shook.

14

A family-run biz since '76,
The perfect spot to get your taco fix,
A brown and orange sign on this small stand,
This James Beard Award winner sure is grand.

____

____

15

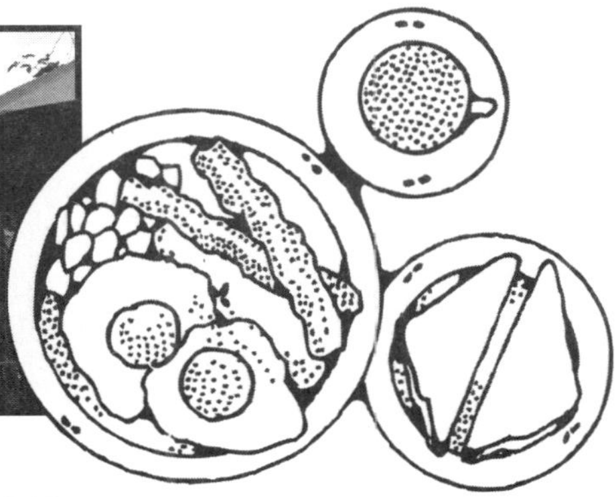

A brunch favorite, not everyone knows
It's built from two historic bungalows.
Namesake recesses hide within the brick,
While a Craftsman in back looks mighty slick.

____

____

16

Mayan-style pyramid, blocks of concrete,
Built by Lloyd Wright, can be seen from the street.
Secrets reside behind the copper gate,
Could it be linked to the Black Dahlia's fate?

17

A bronze cub from the people of Berlin,
With paws out, this statue welcomes you in
To LA's largest park next to its name,
It seems to be dancing: clearly quite tame.

18

These four angels mark both sides of Thai Town,
But you won't see them if you're looking down.
These mythic creatures protect and stand guard,
Half woman, half lion, in gold, unmarred.

19

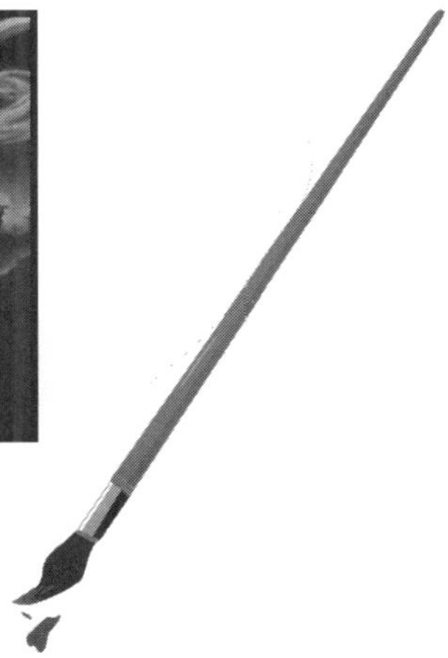

A haunting scene depicted on the wall,
Events of 1915 will appall.
Tribute to Armenian lives taken,
Chained hands, grim faces, you'll leave quite shaken.

Hollywood

While Hollywood may seem like a larger-than-life symbol of the entertainment industry, it's also a bustling neighborhood just west of Los Feliz. LA's film industry really began in an area once known as Edendale (parts of Los Feliz, Silver Lake, and Echo Park), yet Hollywood (aka Tinseltown) soon became its epicenter. Most of the major studios have since moved elsewhere (save for Paramount), but you'll still find plenty of fun Hollywood history to explore here, plus legendary theaters and hotels, and classic restaurants and bars. Most landmarks can be found near and on Hollywood and Sunset boulevards. Take the Metro B Line (Red) to Hollywood/Highland. Metered parking and lots are available.

1

It's not easy being green way up there,
But dressed as the Tramp, Kermit has no care.
Chaplin himself peers from a faux door,
Once his studio, now Muppets galore.

2

A deco steel gazebo with a spire,
Held up by four actresses that inspire.
Marilyn was stolen from the spire's peak,
But find the King and Fab Four if you seek.

3

Named after the 26th president,
For the first Oscars, here's where the stars went,
Arched windows and Churrigueresque details,
Hockney pool and all the Hollywood tales.

4

Up the hill, a fortress if you believe,
This Victorian has tricks up its sleeve.
A clubhouse once known as Holly Chateau,
Full of illusions for those in the know.

5

Its forecourt is a film geek's obsession:
Norma Talmadge left the first impression,
Imported from China, "heaven dogs" guard
Sid's famous theater, to miss it is hard.

6

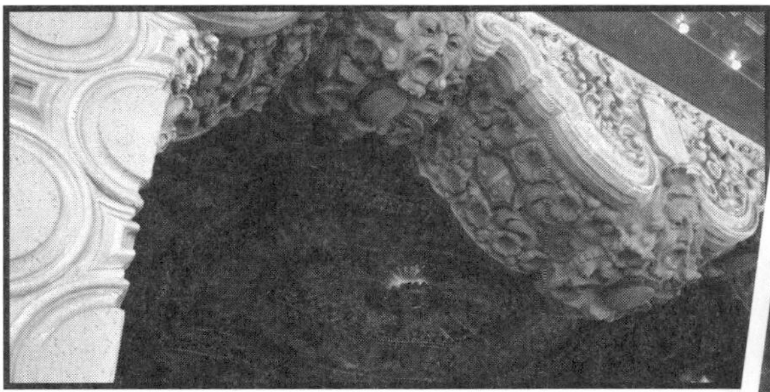

It shares a name with Yosemite's rock,
By the box office, baroque faces gawk,
Hosted the premiere of *Citizen Kane*,
There's now live stage shows, where Disney films reign.

7

The only star not on the ground you'll see
Floats like a butterfly, stings like a bee;
Of thousands of stars on the Walk of Fame,
Head to the Dolby for the Greatest's name.

8

An art deco building in pink and gray,
Tall windows with a marble entryway,
Where golden era stars got their makeup,
Now see movie memorabilia close-up.

9

Plaster reliefs and marquee still reveal
A dancing hog with more whistle than squeal,
The last outpost of a historic chain,
But efforts to preserve have been in vain.

10

Hieroglyphics adorn this grand courtyard,
On tiled roof, costumed actors once stood guard,
Hosted Hollywood's first movie premiere,
New and classic films can still be seen here.

11

A green sign with neon leads to the door,
Hollywood's oldest, with stories galore,
For classic dining since 1919,
Since Chaplin, the place to see and be seen.

12

Spanish colonial down Cherokee,
Leafy ironwork with a balcony,
A haunted watering hole loved by stars,
You've found one of Hollywood's oldest bars.

13

This streamline building is shaped like a ship,
With a globe-topped tower, it's hard to skip.
Surrounded by buildings with worldly flair,
Once stylish shops, now offices are there.

14

Hollywood's tallest building for a time,
Golden era stars stayed fit in their prime,
The first Emmy Awards were hosted here,
A legendary club, that much is clear.

15

The world's first concrete geodesic dome,
Three hundred hexagons like honeycomb.
Inside, a curved screen for three projectors,
An icon loved by fans and directors.

16

A Sheets mosaic of stars worth saving,
Famous names in black marble engraving,
Hollywood's first feature filmed on this site,
Stained glass in back really catches the light.

17

The last palace built for a vaudeville chain,
Above the marquee, Mayan figures reign.
Movies once screened beneath the gold tower,
Live theater once again has its hour.

18

The world's first circular office tower,
There's a mural of musical power,
Blinking light spells "Hollywood" in Morse code,
For the stars of today, Nat paved the road.

19

A shingled roof that's set back from the cars,
This Queen Anne was school for kids of the stars.
It's Hollywood's oldest home that still stands,
Now a speakeasy bar with shows and bands.

North Hollywood

Just north of Studio City and west of Burbank, North Hollywood offers a great starting point for exploring the vast San Fernando Valley. This scavenger hunt is focused on the North Hollywood (or NoHo) Arts District, particularly Lankershim Boulevard, which is an easily accessible area with historic buildings, performing arts theaters, and cool restaurants and bars. Take the Metro B Line (Red) or the G Line (Orange) bus. Free and metered parking is available.

1

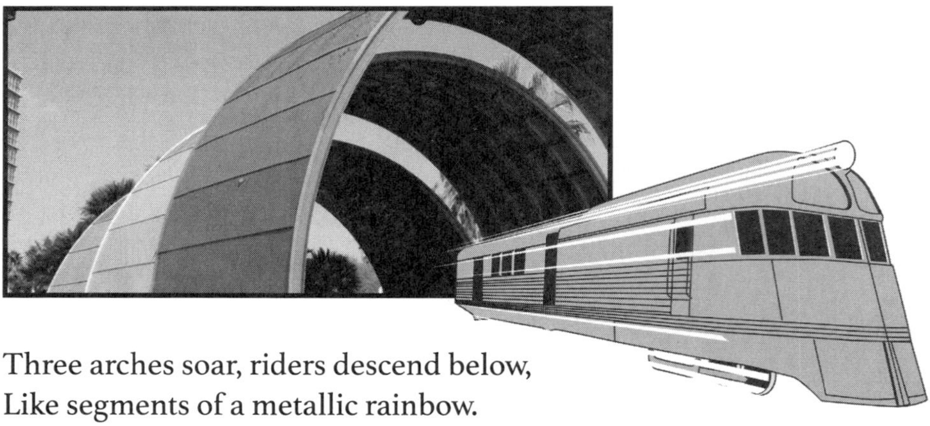

Three arches soar, riders descend below,
Like segments of a metallic rainbow.
Kaleidoscope of history downstairs,
See the region's past hand-painted on squares.

2

Built in 1896 to ship fruit,
Then, as a Red Car stop, to commute,
Mustard yellow with brown trim, now restored,
For a fresh cup of coffee, all aboard!

3

Red brick with classical details in stone,
NoHo's first bank, where you could get a loan.
Now you'll find food, drinks, and music at night,
Look for the red and yellow neon light.

4

Something old, something blue, restored like new,
Next door, a fountain, colorful art, too,
One of NoHo's founders once called it home,
Almost lost, now through history you can comb.

5

An eagle crest with two soldiers, each side,
Above the deco and neon, they hide,
First opened for silents and vaudeville shows,
Once again, where the theater lover goes.

6

Designed like dining cars that rode the rails,
It's still cooking, with historic details,
Started serving in 1926,
Now it's the place to get your waffle kicks.

7

An atom held by the winged muse of art,
Massive award for those who played their part.
Nearby, the faces of small-screen icons,
A Hall of Fame Garden, legends in bronze.

8

This famous pilot once lived near NoHo,
First woman to cross Atlantic solo,
Cast in bronze with a propeller in hand,
Near her namesake library, see her stand.

9

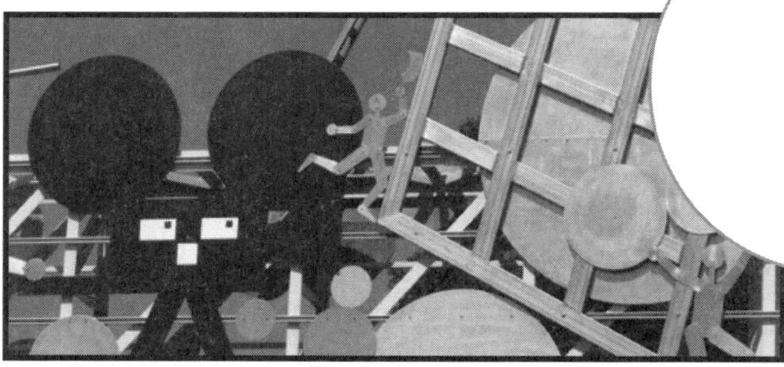

A yellow-green frame spans above the street,
As you head north, this welcome sign will greet,
Houses perched high, circles 'round the nickname,
Winged figures and creatives on the frame.

10

A giant barrel built in '41,
Roadside architecture designed for fun,
Now restored, and there's a bulldog behind,
The clock in front says it's time to unwind.

11

Idols guard the door, a thatch roof above,
A place that fans of tropical drinks love.
Neon and four torches light up the night,
In this house of kitsch, flaming drinks shine bright.

Koreatown

Just west of Westlake and Downtown and south of Hollywood, Koreatown is a vibrant and diverse, historic neighborhood. The area is packed with a fantastic variety of Korean restaurants, bars (including lots of karaoke), shops, and spas, plus Oaxacan and Salvadoran eateries. Much of this hunt takes place along and around Wilshire Boulevard, which saw rapid growth in the early 20th century, so many stops include former Old Hollywood haunts, art deco landmarks, and historic social clubs. Take the Metro B Line (Red) or D Line (Purple) to Wilshire/Vermont or the D Line to Wilshire/Western. Metered street parking and lots are available.

1

A women's club since 1894,
Don't miss the E above the iron door.
Designed after Italian Renaissance,
That is, except for rooftop neon fonts.

2

A monument designed by Millard Sheets,
It's dedicated to masonic feats.
Large figures tell how each one played their part,
Now it's used for contemporary art.

3

With balconies that Juliet would love
And neon signs to catch your eye above,
It's been home to stars of the stage and screen,
Enjoy its Spanish style and windows green.

4

Turquoise terra-cotta tiles soar so high,
Art deco chevrons help to trick the eye.
Twin blade signs and a marquee say its name,
Almost torn down: it would have been a shame.

5

The name of this small park might ring a bell,
Those that made Philly's made this one as well,
Community fought to keep this space green,
Korean broadcaster is also seen.

6

LA's oldest Jewish congregation,
Beneath the dome meets for celebration,
Hollywood helped build Pantheon-like site,
Its geometric event space shines bright.

7

Was once a bungalow, this holy space;
Now a soaring tower stands in its place.
Romanesque in style with a rose window,
It's now an oasis for those who go.

8

Here's where the stars would come to play and stay,
A grove of "cocoanuts" back in the day.
Although the hotel is long gone from here,
A fountain and a frieze are still held dear.

9

It's now just a dome tucked up on the roof,
But of a derby that was brown, it's proof.
Though long since closed, go upstairs to greet
A place where golden era stars would eat.

10

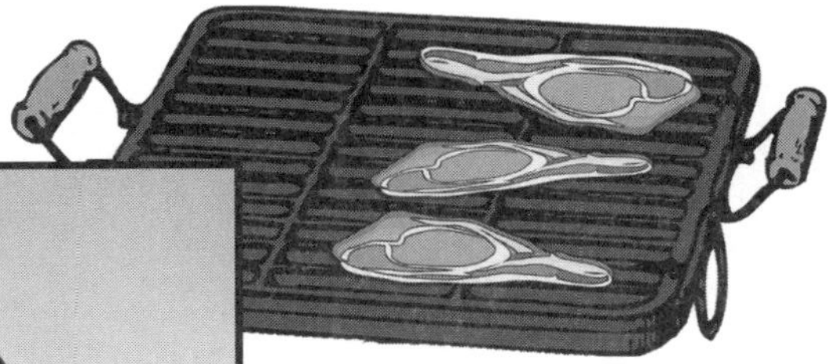

Among the first markets designed for cars,
Now find Korean barbecue and bars.
Just like a castle full of Spanish flair,
Pass through the tunnels to the courtyard square.

11

They're thought to be named for Wilshire's founder,
These apartments' style will never flounder.
Its bar's named for a mutiny at sea,
Where stars have enjoyed food and grog with glee.

12

With floral reliefs and orange-red tile,
This art deco gem was restored with style.
Once a showroom for furs and pianos,
It's now a restaurant whose subtle sign glows.

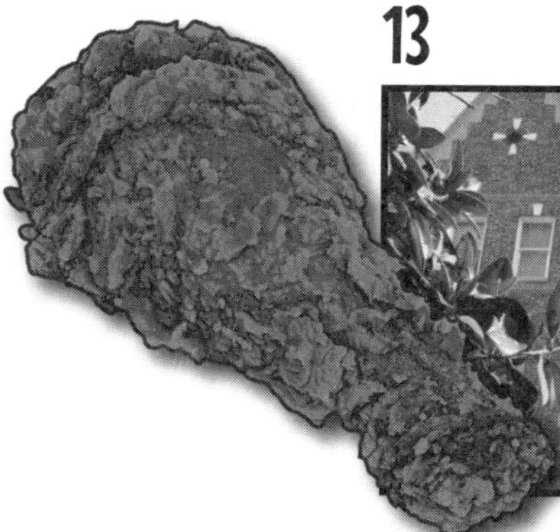

13

Just south of Wilshire hides this royal place,
Korean fried chicken, dimly lit space,
Tudor Revival, apartments above,
Find the red door for vintage vibes you'll love.

14

A silent film star lived on the 10th floor
Where balconies made her hard to ignore.
From her, the classy building gets its name,
This grand brick tower still looks much the same.

15

Once the most glamorous department store,
It's now where law students go to learn more.
Deco designs and terra-cotta tiles,
Its verdigris spire can be seen for miles.

Leimert Park

Located southwest of Downtown and east of Culver City, the historic neighborhood of Leimert Park is a thriving center of Black culture and businesses. Created by Walter H. Leimert in 1927 as one of LA's first planned communities, the area ironically was restricted to white residents until 1948. Most of the landmarks you'll explore are centered around Degnan Boulevard and Leimert Park Plaza, and along the way, you'll encounter exciting art and music venues, excellent food, and bustling shops. Take the Metro K Line to Leimert Park. Free and metered street parking is available.

1

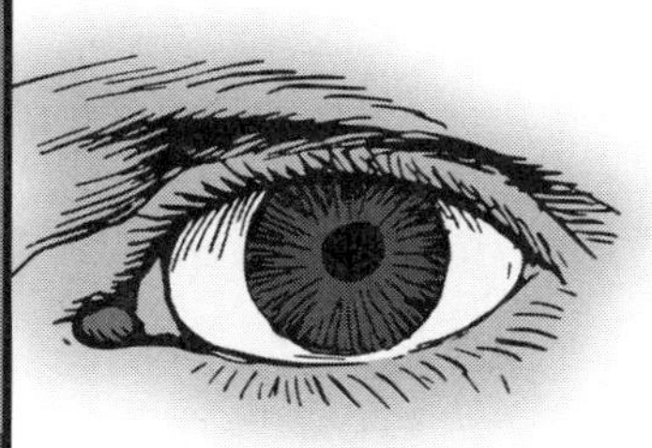

The nine-story tower is quite a "sight,"
Soon the neon will be lit up at night,
Spanish deco in a seafoam green hue,
The rebirth of a historic venue.

2

Cascading water pours down from the bowl,
The plaza where it sits plays a huge role,
Surrounded by green, it's found at the heart
Of a park for music, protest, and art.

3

The brown façade on the corner tells time,
Inside, the space sets a new paradigm.
Museum-curated exhibits are free,
Public programs and foster youth are key.

4

A large eye in mosaic can be seen
As you enter this shop owned by "the Queen."
Custom clothing in vibrant prints in store,
Artwork and jewelry, gifts, drums, and more.

5

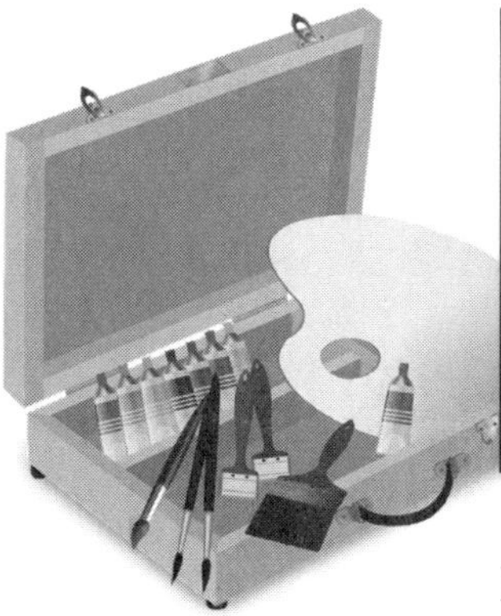

Last bay window on the left, tiles in red,
A place for public programs you'll be led.
Once the home of the Brockman Gallery,
It's still home to art, plus workshops you'll see.

6

Arched window and an awning with a mask,
For nose piercings, this is the place to ask.
Its namesake owner often sits outside,
Handmade jewelry and more, he's your guide.

7

Outside of Hot and Cool, it's on the wall,
With these words, the community won't fall.
African images of resistance,
Lessons for community persistence.

8

It's Amharic for "water over rocks,"
For education, it holds building blocks.
From history to poems, the shelves are lined,
The greats of Black literature you'll find.

9

Artwork in purple and gold gives a clue
To what this performance space offers you.
Wood sign above, LED runs below,
For great poetry and jazz, catch a show.

10

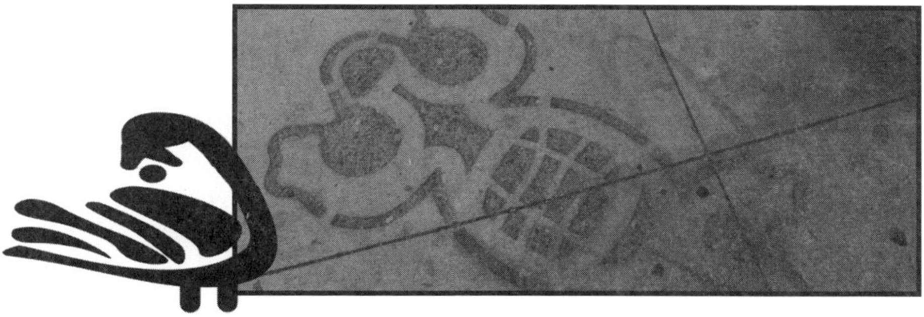

Square plaques embedded where sidewalk is paved,
Surrounded by symbols of those enslaved,
Named for a mythic bird, honored in bronze,
A pathway that celebrates Black icons.

11

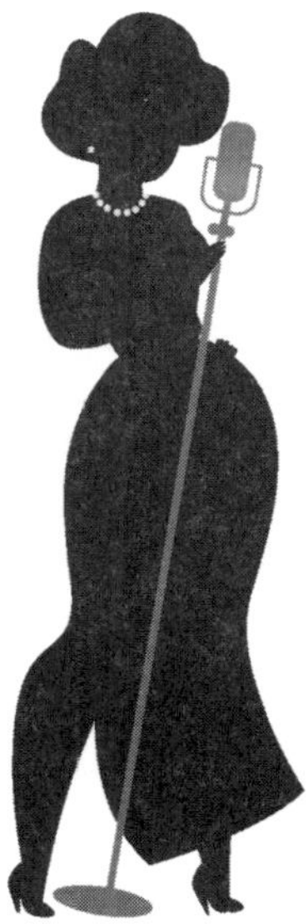

Named for a legend who sang jazz and blues
Where up-and-coming artists pay their dues,
Green awning, the corner of 43rd,
Incredible live music can be heard.

Miracle Mile

West of Koreatown and south of the Fairfax District, Miracle Mile is a historic stretch of Wilshire Boulevard that features major museums, prehistoric sites, and art deco and streamline moderne architecture. What had been a dirt trail, surrounded by oil wells and barley fields, miraculously became a glitzy, car-centric strip of high-end shopping and culture. Some of your search will take you down Fairfax Avenue, so be sure to head a little farther south to check out the great restaurants of Little Ethiopia. Take Metro Bus 216 or 786 or DASH Fairfax to Wilshire and Fairfax.

1

The Old Horseshoe Tavern was once its name,
Now Irish coffee is its claim to fame.
Ivy-covered brick, neon that shines bright,
This Tudor-style pub's shamrock glows at night.

____

____

2

I'm sad to say there is no cup of joe,
But this Googie-style shop is one you know,
Countless movies and shows have filmed in there,
The slanted roof and neon give it flair.

3

Ribbons of steel soar just above your head,
Encircling concrete that glows in red,
The place to go if you feel need for speed,
The home for classics with power of steed.

4

The gold-tiled cylinder gleams in the sun,
Once known as May, the place for a bargain,
A symbol of streamline moderne design,
It's now where all things Oscar are enshrined.

5

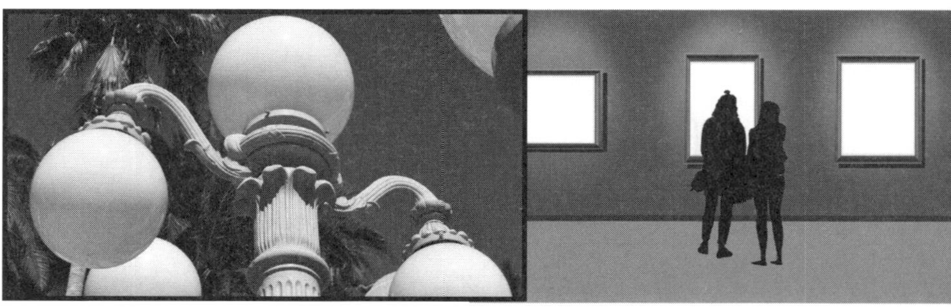

They lit the streets a hundred years ago,
Now grouped together, standing all aglow,
Tall, urban columns are neatly aligned,
Make your way through them, and more art you'll find.

6

Cut from a quarry 100 miles off,
It sits precariously on a trough.
At 300 tons, it's far from lightweight,
Yet this megalith seems to levitate.

7

This old wall once divided East from West,
To trying times, its artwork can attest,
Ten sections wide and 40 in all,
Now works of art commemorate its fall.

8

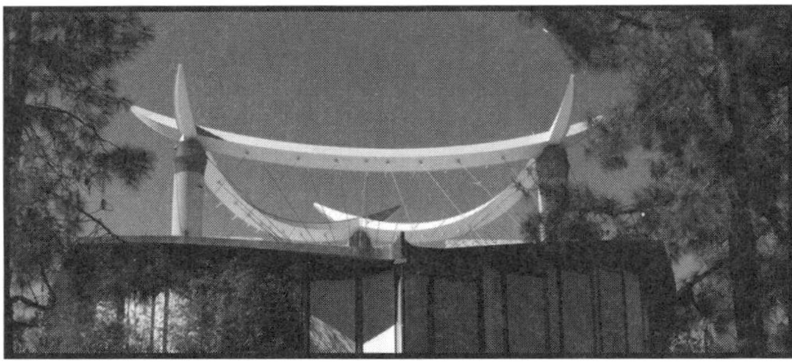

Three mastodon-tusklike shapes on the top,
Sweeping roof and stone pillar, worth a stop,
Translucent, shoji-like screens filter light,
So that artwork inside is seen just right.

9

Ancient asphalt bubbles up from the ground
Where sloths and mammoths long ago were drowned,
The only active Ice Age fossil site
Within a city, and it's quite a sight.

10

While the building style is French Provincial,
If you love to craft, it's simply blissful.
It started as a restaurant that had art,
Now workshops and exhibits play their part.

11

The wisdom to know and courage to do,
His vision, indeed, a miracle, too,
Though all that we see is just a small bust,
He paved a mile gold that once had been dust.

12

An icon of art deco and streamline,
At night it's hard to miss the neon shine,
Though once home to the stars of silver screen,
It's now where up-and-coming bands are seen.

13

Wilshire's first tall tower has a curved base,
And for stylish shoppers, this was the place,
Bearded figures stand guard above the door,
Figures holding snakes are hard to ignore.

14

This façade looks like the things it once sold,
To catch the eye of shutterbugs, it's bold,
And while you can still peer inside the lens,
It's now a place to eat and drink with friends.

15

Opulent terra-cotta, once a bank,
Tall windows and neon sign on its flank,
One of the last decos in black and gold,
Same designers as Richfield Oil of old.

Fairfax District

With West Hollywood to the north and Miracle Mile to the south, the Fairfax district is a charming neighborhood full of great food, shopping, and culture. You'll find trendy and old-school dining options, coveted sneaker stores and vintage clothing shops, and beloved movie theaters. The area is also rich in Jewish American culture and history. Most landmarks are located along Fairfax Avenue, Beverly Boulevard, and Melrose and La Brea avenues, with an initial detour near 3rd Street. Catch Metro Bus 16 or 217 or DASH Fairfax to Fairfax Boulevard and 3rd Street. Metered and free parking is available.

1

Yellow canopy, lions on the flank,
Vintage pumps where you could once fill your tank.
Before the farmers, there were oil fields here,
This replica makes the history clear.

2

Reaching out a hand to help those in need,
Tall steel wings surround this heroic Swede,
Saved thousands from death camps in World War II,
Yet later held as a prisoner, too.

3

Streamline moderne tower in green and white.
Tribute to the venue once on this site,
Sports, Ice Capades, and even Elvis played,
Lost to fire, now a park offers shade.

4

Six granite pillars, 18 feet high, black,
For six million killed, resembles smokestack.
Underground museum, first of its kind,
Horrors committed, it serves to remind.

____

____

5

A tall sign for this iconic deli,
Pastrami and matzo fill your belly,
First opened in Boyle Heights, runs 'round the clock,
Its Kibitz Room loved by legends of rock.

____

____

6

Three posters and a curved window you'll see,
Arthouse and classic films on the marquee,
Debuted with silent films in '42,
Now you'll find movies, food, and clothing, too.

7

Named for a lord, a lion on the crest,
Its tiled rotunda stands out from the rest,
A school for agriculture years ago,
Sunday market helps students: you should go.

8

Began as a pushcart in '39,
Its vibrant, namesake color on the sign,
A Hollywood favorite, lines down the block,
Hard to resist the chili dogs they hawk.

9

Orange, yellow, and red stripes, globe lights on top,
For film fans, this is an essential stop.
The venue's lived many lives through the years,
Now owned by Tarantino, still brings cheers.

10

Iconic red neon calls out at night,
Like its namesake, you'll want to take a bite,
Colorful windows, benches for long waits,
Strong margaritas and Mexican plates.

____

____

11

Gothic-style castle with drawbridge and moat;
Of the name in the turret's arch, take note,
Built with bricks from LA's third City Hall,
For Pantages and more, painted the wall.

____

____

West Hollywood

An independent city with plenty of personality, West Hollywood is located east of Beverly Hills and north of the Fairfax District. This scavenger hunt covers two of the area's busiest sections: Santa Monica Boulevard, featuring old-school Hollywood haunts and thriving LGBTQ venues and historic sites; and the iconic Sunset Strip with its legendary music venues, classic hotels, and quirky eateries. Catch Metro Bus 2 or 218 to Sunset/ Crescent Heights or the 4 to Santa Monica/Formosa. There are also free Cityline Shuttles Monday through Saturday during the day and the free WeHo PickUp trolley along Santa Monica Boulevard on weekend nights. Metered street parking and lots are available.

1

Green and red awnings, façade a deep red,
Through historic doors, countless stars have tread,
Vintage red car trolley seen from the side,
Even mobsters found it a place to hide.

2

Vintage camera stands outside of the lot,
A tilting skyline where PickFair films shot.
In the garage where Howard Hughes would park,
See a historic workshop in the dark.

3

Its namesake server holds out a platter,
There's pride here, where more than burgers matter,
Beneath the neon sign and rainbow flag.
To miss bingo and brunch would be a drag.

4

Water cascades from an inverted cone,
Five shields for armed forces, carved out of stone,
Four flagpoles and green space to sit and reflect,
Honors those who served where streets intersect.

5

A bun and a dog restored from the past,
An iconic stand reopened at last.
Snappy dogs since '46, quite the tale,
And for fans of The Doors, a fun detail.

6

Stained glass windows, terra-cotta creatures,
Baked goods and dancing with church-like features,
It's now an LGBTQ landmark
That helped bring gay nightlife out of the dark.

7

Red, green, and blue dominate the skyline,
Geometric glass, in the light they shine,
Home to showrooms and workshops, lots of style,
They are loved by some, while others revile.

8

The windows are framed with green deco trim
The curved corner in front makes it look slim.
Gallery for a historic archive,
Here, LGBTQ exhibits thrive.

9

Built of logs for scouts a long time ago,
Gable above the porch, door down below,
It looks like it belongs deep in the wood,
Support services now do a lot of good.

10

Bright yellow bungalow beloved by stars,
Under green neon glow, lineup of cars,
Once known as Domenico's, horseshoe-shaped sign,
Since '64, great red sauce and wine.

11

For traveling musicians, it's a home,
Like wandering minstrels, here's where they roam.
Through the tavern door beneath the orange sign,
Fans of all genres nightly form a line.

12

A castle on high for celebs with dough,
If you must get in trouble, here's where to go.
The striped awnings protect stars from the sun,
Tall walls hide rumors of mischief and fun.

13

It's all aboard for these classic wieners,
Loaded with chili: might need the cleaners.
This Union Pacific passenger car
Now shines in yellow, a Sunset Strip star.

14

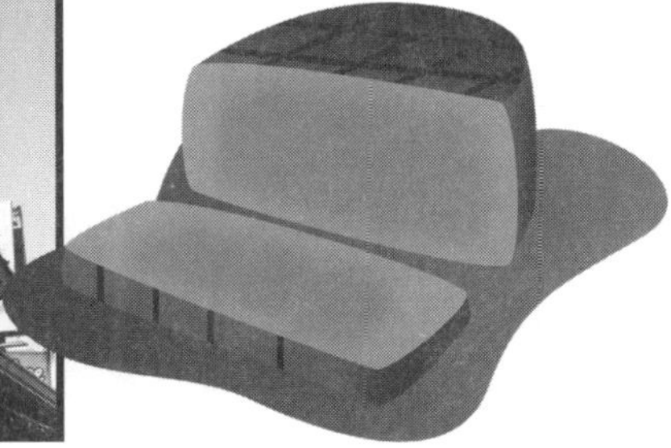

You might think you've traveled to the Wild West,
Judging by how the mannequins are dressed.
Strong drinks and the steaks no doubt have their pull,
But crowds come for the mechanical bull.

15

Art deco towers soar above Sunset,
Where the Devil, Adam, and Eve have met,
Once home to Sinatra, Monroe, and Wayne,
It's now a hotel, but celebs still reign.

16

Laughter is the thing to buy at this store,
You'll sit, they'll stand, and they'll try not to bore.
Once home to iconic restaurant Ciro's,
"Paid regulars'" names are comic heroes.

17

Venetian Renaissance, ornate design,
Above a fountain, two stairways align.
Once home to stars as Hacienda Park,
Now a restaurant where celebs disembark.

18

A-frame Googie roof and bright neon sign,
This retro joint is where night owls can dine.
Once known as Ben Frank's, where bands would hang out,
Most are now on the jukeboxes found throughout.

19

Bright green flying saucer, arched windows pink,
Designed by Oscar Niemeyer, many think,
First a cosmetic surgeon's office space,
Now the cofounder of Devo's workplace.

20

A literary landmark long held dear,
Both the great and the infamous shop here.
Name in neon, wooden signpost above,
Since '75, an indie to love.

21

Oldest live music venue on the Strip,
Opened '64, made a dance craze hip,
Red and black on the corner, once a bank,
Many rock legends have this place to thank.

22

Streamline marquee, its name in neon lights,
When it opened, Neil Young played the first nights.
Once a market, then a burlesque nightclub,
Five decades ago, became a rock hub.

23

Once known as the Villa Nova restaurant,
From movie stars to a rock-and-roll haunt.
Find the names of rock icons carved in brick,
Somewhere over the roof, the name will click.

Beverly Hills

With West Hollywood to the northeast and Westwood to the west, Beverly Hills is a destination with a worldwide reputation for its celebrity-dotted zip code and glamorous Rodeo Drive. But the city also features fascinating public art and notable architecture, beautiful parks and fountains, cultural institutions, and great restaurants. While much of your search will take place within the triangle of Wilshire Boulevard, Rexford Drive, and Santa Monica Boulevard, you'll also venture northwest into "the Flats." Take Metro Bus 20, 720, or 786 to Wilshire/Rodeo. Metered street parking and city lots are available.

1

Built on the site of a former raceway,
Guests can play *Pretty Woman* for a day.
Elvis and other stars helped make it cool,
Find wild creatures above the vestibule.

2

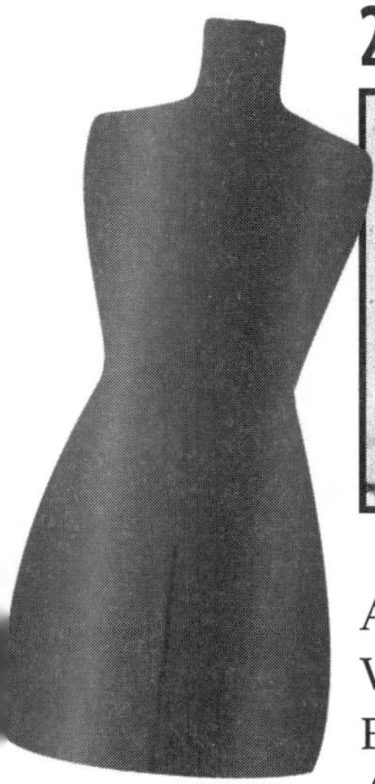

A silver torso is the start of this walk,
Which honors fashion icons along the block.
Embedded bronze plaques with style's biggest names,
Autographs and quotes within these square frames.

3

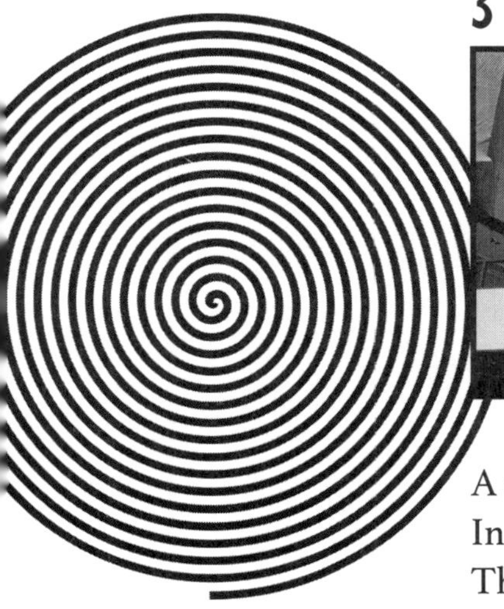

A spiral ramp designed to let in light
In the heart of Rodeo: Frank Lloyd Wright.
The streamline spire like a tree to trim,
SoCal's only non-residence from him.

4

Beloved Jewish deli since '45,
With its orange sign, continues to thrive,
A favorite spot for stars and locals, too,
Hungry? A pastrami on rye will do.

5

It's about as old as Beverly Hills,
More shade than a palm tree, without the frills,
Its mammoth trunk stands just west of the pond,
Look for its plaque and soon you'll grow quite fond.

6

The sign behind is perfect for a pose,
In the pond below, just don't dip your toes.
First built over a hundred years ago,
Now restored, the floating flowers can grow.

7

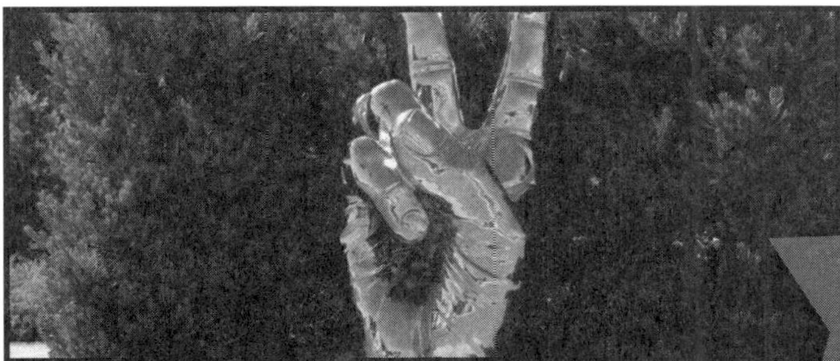

This 800-pound steel is eight feet tall,
Designed by a Beatle, it wasn't Paul,
To his backbeat he hopes you will still dance,
With this gesture, give peace and love a chance.

8

Built on the site of a railway station,
It brought in mail from across the nation.
Italian Renaissance, terra-cotta trim,
Now the show starts when the house lights dim.

9

Gilded cupola, dome of vibrant tiles,
Its eight-story tower is seen for miles,
Since '32, the heart of civic life,
To lose its Spanish style would cause much strife.

10

Thirty-foot salvaged beam from Ground Zero,
Names of the dead and each fallen hero,
Pentagon shape and Twin Towers in stone,
A place to sit with others or alone.

11

Its canopy swoops just like a spaceship,
Filling your tank has never been so hip.
Googie-style roof with orange squares, so retro,
Meant for LAX, moved here long ago.

12

A pond with a bridge and flowers that bloom,
You might think the owner rides on a broom.
Built for silent film with storybook style,
Its wicked look makes trick-or-treaters smile.

13

A rainbow of colors lights up at night,
As the water rains down, it's quite a sight,
Native American kneels in prayer,
California's history is seen here.

14

Once the front lawn of the big pink hotel,
The first public park, there's roses to smell,
Named for a humorist and star of screen,
As honorary mayor he was seen.

15

Built in 1912, a palace in pink,
Instead of polo, stars come for a drink.
It opened before its namesake city,
Trimmed with green and white, it's still quite pretty.

Westwood Village

Located just west of Beverly Hills and a bit north of Culver City, Westwood Village is a quaint and historic neighborhood, probably best known for its largest resident: the University of California, Los Angeles (UCLA). The area was developed in the 1920s as a Mediterranean-inspired shopping and dining area at the foot of the sprawling university. While it's still popular among students, the neighborhood also offers visitors and locals plenty of excellent restaurants and cultural attractions, including museums, historic theaters, and hidden gardens. Be sure to also explore Westwood Boulevard south of Wilshire Boulevard for one clue, and the area known as Tehrangeles for a myriad of Persian and Iranian restaurants and shops. Take Metro Bus 20 or the Culver City Bus Line 6 to Wilshire/Western. Lots and metered street parking are available.

1

This cylindrical corner with framed doors
Was one of the first Ralph's grocery stores.
As a theater, Rocky Horror debuted;
Beneath the tiles now, coffee perks the mood.

2

An iconic dome, trimmed with gold, zigzag blue,
Octagonal shape, a portico, too,
Once home to UCLA's first men's dorm,
Now there's food within this historic form.

3

Just like Paris, 1872,
Water poured from the dome when it was new.
There's four maidens: Kindness and Charity,
Plus, Sobriety and Simplicity.

4

A crest with a crown on the corner in stone,
Two colonial faces, names unknown,
Wood latticework windows, if you discern,
Designed by Clements, known for the Wiltern.

5

Once known as the Fox, built in '31,
Wedding cake tower, a beacon for fun,
Beneath its high columns, griffins roar,
A distinctive marquee, premieres galore.

6

Named for the mascot of UCLA,
A wraparound marquee shows what will play,
Streamline moderne designed by S. Charles Lee,
Blue-gold neon, terrazzo floor to see.

7

Ivy-covered walls, roof of orange tile,
Fountain in the courtyard, plenty of style.
A Masonic clubhouse in '29,
Now performances on stage truly shine.

8

An entry of glass bricks, lines down the block,
To this institution, sweet tooths will flock,
Fresh cookies and ice cream: the perfect pair,
Named for grandma, prices are still low here.

9

East of campus, a living museum,
You'll marvel at these plants when you see 'em,
Thousands of species from around the world,
Explore for free to have mysteries unfurled.

10

In '33, known as "Talk of the Town,"
Its rotunda loved by stars of renown,
A 30-foot glass dome catches the eye,
In the restaurant, a ficus grows sky-high.

11

South of Wilshire, down Glendon, an alley,
Famous grounds where stars had their finale.
Kisses for Marilyn, fun epitaphs,
Tombstones look like Hollywood autographs.

Culver City

Northeast of Venice and southwest of Miracle Mile, Culver City has a long moviemaking history and a lively downtown perfect for strolling. Founded in 1917 as the vision of its namesake, Harry Culver, the city soon became home to several early movie studios, dubbing itself "the Heart of Screenland." You'll still find those historic lots under different names now, along with an exciting mix of restaurants, unexpected museums, theaters, and lots of public art and murals. Most of these landmarks can be found along Culver and Venice boulevards, with a few that stretch on either side of the downtown area. Take the Metro E Line (Expo) to Culver City. Several city parking lots and metered spots are available.

1

Loaves for Olympians were once baked here,
Angelenos long held their baked goods dear.
Yellow coaches once delivered the bread,
Now home to designers and food instead.

2

This mission revival you shouldn't skip,
It powered the Balloon Route Trolley Trip.
Though the power lines are now just for show,
The actors inside you should get to know.

3

A waterless fountain, a scroll-like sign,
Between fact and fiction, it blurs the line,
A glass-covered nook is by the front door,
It hints at the mysteries this place holds in store.

4

Flowers in concrete adorn the archway,
The news was printed here back in the day.
Reborn as a food hall, there's treats in store,
Just look for the flagpole above the door.

5

This comic pair often filmed on Main Street,
But check the alley behind for a treat:
Holding a hammer and in black and white,
This art's best seen from parking structure height.

6

Cinematic mansion, first on the lot,
Where *Gone with the Wind* and others were shot.
Rosebuds lead to tall, white pillars in front,
Inspired by Mount Vernon, worth the hunt.

____

____

7

Culver's first "skyscraper" back in the day,
Here, silver-screen stars and Munchkins would stay,
Red and green designs hide up in the eaves,
Flatiron with ghost stories up its sleeves.

____

____

8

Culver's namesake in bronze, reading the news,
Grab a seat on the bench, but just don't snooze,
Harry's dream became a reality;
His wife and daughter stand behind with glee.

9

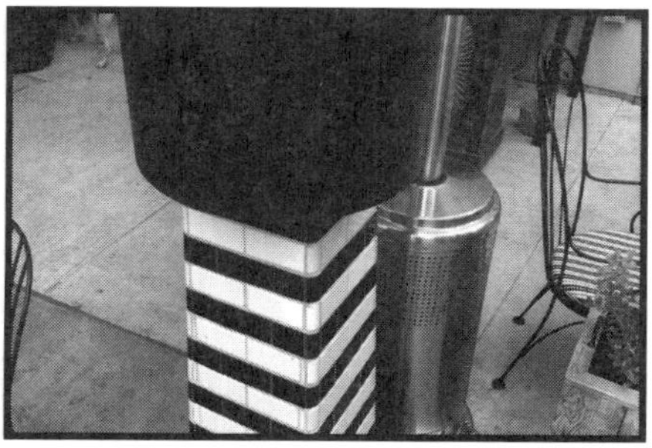

Seven pedestals with drums you can spin
To witness a moving image within.
First invented in 1834,
Screenland tributes found around downtown's core.

10

You'll love this famous pair behind the wheel,
TV pioneers, made us laugh and feel,
In the back seat, the drum from Babalú,
And just down the road, you'll see Desilu.

11

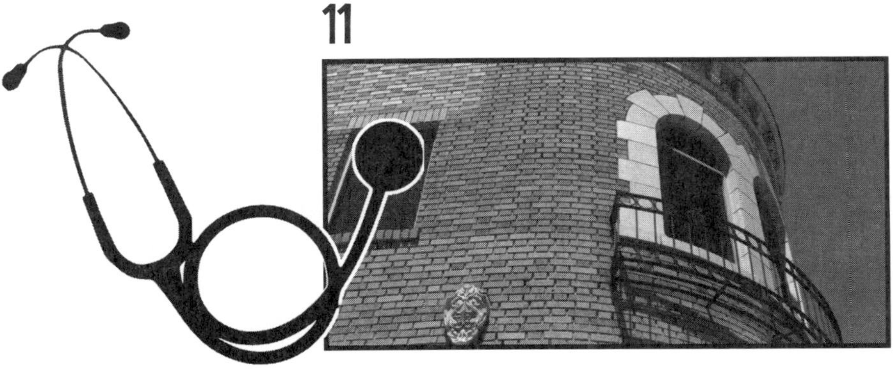

Neoclassical arches, rose-tan brick,
Culver's first hospital cared for the sick,
Two eye-like windows above the front door.
You'll now find a restaurant on the first floor.

12

Swirls and scrolls from box office to tower,
Neon lights when they turn on the power.
Before a show, note the terrazzo floor,
Though once for film, theater's beyond the door.

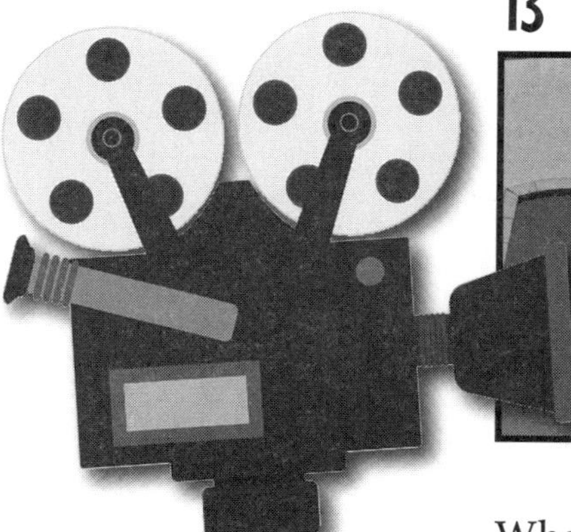

13

What City Hall looked like in '28,
Through the replica façade, art awaits,
Vintage camera, quotes that inspire,
A watery tribute to admire.

14

Spanish colonial, ceramic tiles,
The site of Culver's first pool, which brought smiles,
Once a club for vets and service members,
Now hospital-owned, a plaque remembers.

15

Culver's first church was built upon this site,
Established before the city shone bright.
A small wooden chapel served the people,
Figueroa's land, now a tall steeple.

16

Cute cottages straight from a storybook,
You might see Frodo if you take a look.
Pond of koi and turtles, sweeping rooftop,
Disney artist designed them: worth a stop.

17

Somewhere over Sony's studio lot,
The place where *The Wizard of Oz* was shot,
This colorful steel arch is way up high,
Tony Tasset designed, where bluebirds fly.

18

A place to remember those who have fought,
The tower designed to view the back lot.
In the pool in front, you can't take a dip,
But instead, you will find a swirling strip.

19

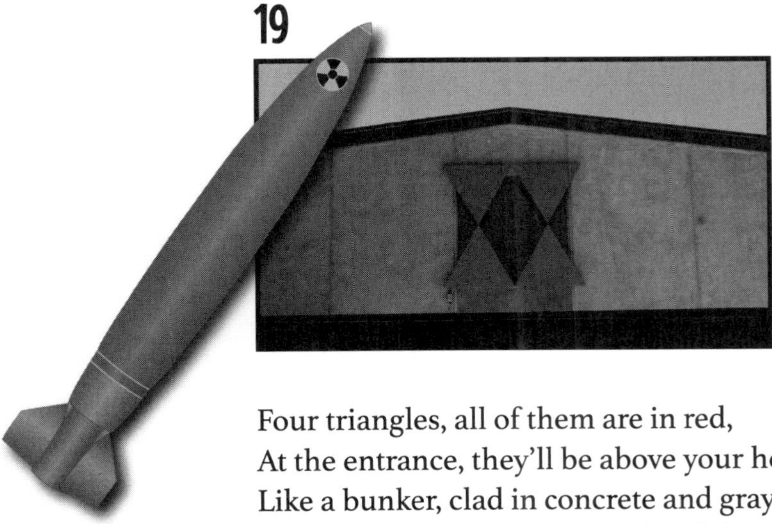

Four triangles, all of them are in red,
At the entrance, they'll be above your head.
Like a bunker, clad in concrete and gray,
To learn about the Cold War, head this way.

Santa Monica

The seaside city of Santa Monica, north of Venice and northwest of Culver City, offers laid-back beach vibes with plenty of history. Among the city's upscale restaurants and hotels, you'll find architectural landmarks and cultural institutions. Your hunt for clues will take you to the iconic Santa Monica Pier and Palisades Park for ocean views, as well as around Downtown Santa Monica and the 3rd Street Promenade, where you'll find bustling shops and restaurants among historic buildings. Be sure to also visit the Santa Monica History Museum. Catch the Metro E Line (Expo) to Downtown Santa Monica. Metered street parking and city lots are available.

1

Santa Monica's founder sits out front,
From the porch of his son's house, start this hunt,
Two chimneys, gray-green Victorian,
Find a California historian.

2

Gabled roof with a small front porch covered,
Narrow Victorian rediscovered.
Three rooms in a row, you could shoot right through,
Here, you'll learn history and take tours, too.

3

The frame of a shotgun house in red steel,
Historic injustice stanzas reveal
Homes burned, a Black community displaced,
Where now a park and public art are placed.

4

Since the '30s, where gymnasts show off skills,
These beachfront rings, bars, and ropes still bring thrills,
Skilled acrobats and fitness pioneers,
Long before Venice, this gym brought the cheers.

5

Moorish windows, octagonal towers,
Beneath blue roof, horses spin for hours,
Built by an amusement park pioneer,
Part of what was his namesake Pleasure Pier.

6

Though you can't drive to it with a carload,
This sign marks the end of the Mother Road.
Just before Pacific Park stands the post,
Symbolic end where the trail meets the coast.

7

Two steel, shell-like shapes offer ocean views,
They're part of a park with paths you can choose.
Rolling hills, shady trees, and public art,
Named for the native tribe here from the start.

8

Square brown façade with a turret on top,
A lens inside makes images flip-flop,
The tripod on the front gives you a clue,
Historic device with 360 view.

9

For decades, the tallest building around,
With a four-sided clock this landmark's crowned,
Twelve-story deco built in '29,
Tall columns and windows where you can dine.

10

Prehistoric pairs parade on the street,
Six can be found where shoppers take a seat,
Covered in ivy, they'll help keep things cool,
Some of them spout water into a pool.

11

Oldest music venue on the Westside,
Vintage windows with imbibers outside.
Drinks were first poured during Prohibition;
Beneath red neon, hear a musician.

12

The oldest brick building, windows rounded,
Built when Santa Monica was founded.
First used as a tavern, then City Hall,
Other occupants written on the wall.

13

The city's namesake is cast in concrete,
The deco sculpture stands at 18 feet.
A Public Works Project from '34,
Long veil with hands crossed, her back to the shore.

14

Eighty feet tall and nearly twice as wide,
Beneath dark green leaves, serpentine roots hide,
Brought by a sailor to settle bar debt,
It keeps growing where hotel guests are met.

15

A redwood structure painted forest green,
Through its windows, ocean views can be seen.
Built in 1912 on the palisade,
Craftsman-style woodwork offers welcome shade.

Venice

South of Santa Monica and west of Culver City, Venice is an eclectic and artsy beachfront neighborhood with a fascinating history. You'll explore wild street art and stunning murals, local flavor and sights on Ocean Front Walk (better known as the Boardwalk), and trendy shops and upscale restaurants along Abbot Kinney Boulevard—named for the founder of Venice of America. You'll also encounter the iconic Venice canals, remnants of Kinney's grand vision for a beach resort, and amusement piers and parks. Take Metro Bus 33 or 333 to Main Street and Grand Avenue.

1

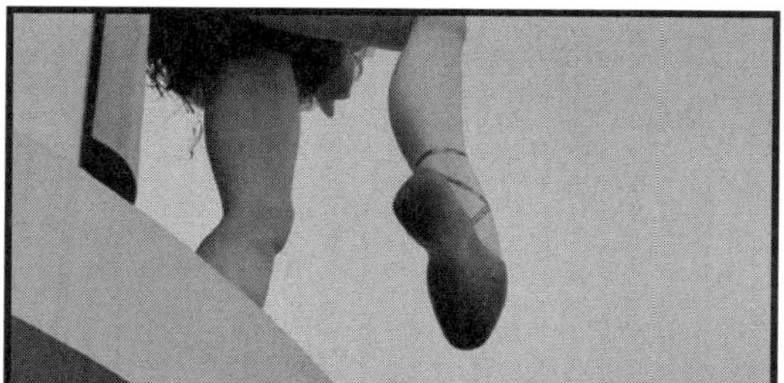

Dancing on a soap box, poised in the light,
Graceful comedian, 30-foot height,
Top hat and tutu, leg designed to swing,
As controversial as *The Rite of Spring.*

2

Between two buildings, field glasses you'll find,
Gehry, Oldenburg, van Bruggen designed,
Giant device used to search far away,
The entrance to a search giant today.

3

A rooster weathervane atop the sign,
See live chickens and veggies on the vine.
An edible landscape for chefs and more,
Workshops and nursery that you'll adore.

4

It's somewhere over the rainbow crosswalk,
Down the alley, past the rooster fish flock,
An orange dome on top of a Queen Anne,
As old as Venice, named for Kinney's plan.

5

Brick building, green trim, built in '25,
LA's oldest clothing label alive.
Chaplin and Fonda wore their overalls,
1895 painted on the walls.

6

This restored blue vessel has seats for two,
Traveled the canals with a singer, too.
Sent from Italy, they'd paddle and croon
When the circle in front was a lagoon.

7

A film noir tribute to Orson Welles,
This mural and street, you'll see parallels,
Colonnade remains, though less than before,
You'll pass them both as you head toward the shore.

8

Strung across the street and lit up at night,
Gateway to the beach, an iconic sight,
The first one installed in 1905,
Proves Abbot Kinney's dream is still alive.

____

____

9

Soaring steel between the beach and boardwalk,
I-beams shaped like Vs are seen down the block,
Sixty feet tall, perched on a grassy hill,
Temporary in '01, but there still.

____

____

10

Remains of an outdoor theater still stand,
Concrete walls and cones of "The Pit" in sand,
Now street artists can work without constraint,
And, with a permit, anyone can paint.

11

From the Z-Boys of Dogtown to today,
Here's where future legends carve the way.
In bowls and on rails, see impressive tricks,
All ages welcome: they're sure to transfix.

12

A red and white awning like the big top,
Find your next beach read in this cozy shop.
Next to a cafe, right on the boardwalk,
Tomes from around the world, always in stock.

13

Where Arnold once pumped iron in the sun,
"The Pen" is still open to anyone,
Bronze barbells all around, one in concrete,
Bleachers for fans, a stage for the athlete.

14

More than just the name of a stylish street,
On this wall, Venice's founder you'll meet,
Fifty feet high and clad in a gray suit,
Created canals and a railroad route.

15

The Venetian inspiration's quite plain:
Though the first were paved over, these remain.
Stroll the bridges or paddle by canoe,
See Kinney's vision and charming homes, too.

HOLLYWOOD
STOP